Digital Technologies and the Evolving African Newsroom

African newsrooms are experiencing the disruptive impact of new digital technologies on the way they generate and disseminate news. Indeed, newsrooms are being forced to adapt in various ways and there are clear dimensions of localised creativity and adaptations by journalists to the digital revolution. In the same way, the influences of digitisation, internet, and social media are changing the informational needs of readers, including how they engage with news. These developments nonetheless remain on the margins of "mainstream" journalism research—very few researchers have sought to qualitatively capture the implications of developments in digital technologies on the routine practices of African journalists, especially in their "natural habitat", the newsroom.

In this light, this edited volume interrogates the changing ecology of news-making in Africa in the context of rapid technological changes in newsrooms as well as in the wider social context of news production. It brings together six contributions drawn from five countries: Mozambique, South Africa, Zimbabwe, Nigeria and Egypt, to explore practices, challenges and professional normative dilemmas emerging with the adoption and appropriation of new technologies. While the studies point to dimensions of *localised* new technology appropriations as defined by the complex socio-political structures in which African journalists operate, they are not rigidly confined to Africa. They are expressly in dialogue with theoretical observations largely emerging from Western scholarship. In this sense, the book goes beyond simply mainstreaming African perspectives, it engages directly with dominant theoretical observations and offers a point of departure for developing what could loosely be branded as an *African digital journalism epistemology*.

This book was originally published as a special issue of *Digital Journalism*.

Hayes Mawindi Mabweazara, PhD, is a Senior Lecturer in Journalism at Falmouth University, UK. He serves on the editorial board of *Digital Journalism* and the *Journal of Alternative and Community Media* (Griffith University). Mabweazara is also Associate Editor for *African Journalism Studies* (Routledge). As well as guest-editing a special issue of *Digital Journalism* 2(1) (2014), on which this book is based, he co-edited a special issue of *Journalism: Theory, Practice & Criticism* 12(6) (2011), themed: "New Media and Journalism Practice in Africa: An Agenda for Research". He also co-edited: *Online Journalism in Africa* (2014) and is currently working on a monograph, titled: *Africa's Mainstream Press in the Digital Era* (2015).

Journalism Studies: Theory and Practice

Series editor: Bob Franklin, *Cardiff School of Journalism, Media and Cultural Studies, Cardiff University, UK*

The journal *Journalism Studies* was established at the turn of the new millennium by Bob Franklin. It was launched in the context of a burgeoning interest in the scholarly study of journalism and an expansive global community of journalism scholars and researchers. The ambition was to provide a forum for the critical discussion and study of journalism as a subject of intellectual inquiry but also an arena of professional practice. Previously, the study of journalism in the UK and much of Europe was a fairly marginal branch of the larger disciplines of media, communication and cultural studies; only a handful of Universities offered degree programmes in the subject. *Journalism Studies* has flourished and succeeded in providing the intended public space for discussion of research on key issues within the field, to the point where in 2007 a sister journal, *Journalism Practice,* was launched to enable an enhanced focus on practice-based issues, as well as foregrounding studies of journalism education, training and professional concerns. Both journals are among the leading ranked journals within the field and publish six issues annually, in electronic and print formats. More recently, 2013 witnessed the launch of a further companion journal *Digital Journalism* to provide a site for scholarly discussion, analysis and responses to the wide ranging implications of digital technologies for the practice and study of journalism. From the outset, the publication of themed issues has been a commitment for all journals. Their purpose is first, to focus on highly significant or neglected areas of the field; second, to facilitate discussion and analysis of important and topical policy issues; and third, to offer readers an especially high quality and closely focused set of essays, analyses and discussions.

The *Journalism Studies: Theory and Practice* book series draws on a wide range of these themed issues from all journals and thereby extends the critical and public forum provided by them. The Editor of the journals works closely with guest editors to ensure that the books achieve relevance for readers and the highest standards of research rigour and academic excellence. The series makes a significant contribution to the field of journalism studies by inviting distinguished scholars, academics and journalism practitioners to discuss and debate the central concerns within the field. It also reaches a wider readership of scholars, students and practitioners across the social sciences, humanities and communication arts, encouraging them to engage critically with, but also to interrogate, the specialist scholarly studies of journalism which this series provides.

Available titles in the series:

Mapping the Magazine: Comparative Studies in Magazine Journalism
Edited by Tim Holmes

The Future of Newspapers
Edited by Bob Franklin

Language and Journalism
Edited by John Richardson

The Future of Journalism
Edited by Bob Franklin

Exploration in Global Media Ethics
Edited by Muhammad Ayish and Shakuntala Rao

Foreign Correspondence
Edited by John Maxwell Hamilton and Regina G. Lawrence

How Journalism Uses History
Edited by Martin Conboy

Lifestyle Journalism
Edited by Folker Hanusch

Environmental Journalism
Edited by Henrik Bødker and Irene Neverla

Online Reporting of Elections
Edited by Einar Thorsen

The Future of Journalism: Developments and Debates
Edited by Bob Franklin

Cross-continental Views on Journalistic Skills
Edited by Leen d'Haenens, Michaël Opgenhaffen and Maarten Corten

Cosmopolitanism and the New News Media
Edited by Lilie Chouliaraki and Bolette Blaagaard

The Press and Popular Culture in Interwar Europe
Edited by Sarah Newman and Matt Houlbrook

Community Journalism Midst Media Revolution
Edited by Sue Robinson

Digital Technologies and the Evolving African Newsroom
Towards an African Digital Journalism Epistemology
Edited by Hayes Mawindi Mabweazara

Digital Technologies and the Evolving African Newsroom

Towards an African Digital Journalism Epistemology

Edited by
Hayes Mawindi Mabweazara

Routledge
Taylor & Francis Group
LONDON AND NEW YORK

First published 2015
by Routledge
2 Park Square, Milton Park, Abingdon, Oxon, OX14 4RN, UK

and by Routledge
711 Third Avenue, New York, NY 10017, USA

First issued in papperback 2017

Routledge is an imprint of the Taylor & Francis Group, an informa business

British Library Cataloguing in Publication Data
A catalogue record for this book is available from the British Library

ISBN 13: 978-1-138-30504-5 (pbk)
ISBN 13: 978-1-138-82383-9 (hbk)

Typeset in Myriad
by RefineCatch Limited, Bungay, Suffolk

Publisher's Note
The publisher accepts responsibility for any inconsistencies that may have arisen during the conversion of this book from journal articles to book chapters, namely the possible inclusion of journal terminology.

Disclaimer
Every effort has been made to contact copyright holders for their permission to reprint material in this book. The publishers would be grateful to hear from any copyright holder who is not here acknowledged and will undertake to rectify any errors or omissions in future editions of this book.

Contents

Citation Information

The chapters in this book were originally published in *Digital Journalism*, volume 2, no. 1, (February 2014). When citing this material, please use the original page numbering for each article, as follows:

Editorial Note

Editorial Note
Bob Franklin
Digital Journalism, volume 2, no. 1 (February 2014) pp. 1

Chapter 1

Introduction: 'Digital technologies and the evolving African newsroom': towards an African digital journalism epistemology
Hayes Mawindi Mabweazara
Digital Journalism, volume 2, no. 1 (February 2014) pp. 2–11

Chapter 2

New Media Technologies and Internal Newsroom Creativity in Mozambique: The case of @verdade
Admire Mare
Digital Journalism, volume 2, no. 1 (February 2014) pp. 12–28

Chapter 3

Social Media and Community Radio Journalism in South Africa
Tanja Bosch
Digital Journalism, volume 2, no. 1 (February 2014) pp. 29–43

Chapter 4

Readers Comments on Zimbabwean Newspaper Websites: How audience voices are challenging and (re)defining traditional journalism
Hayes Mawindi Mabweazara
Digital Journalism, volume 2, no. 1 (February 2014) pp. 44–61

Chapter 5

Negotiating Convergence: "Alternative" journalism and institutional practices of Nigerian journalists
Motilola Olufenwa Akinfemisoye
Digital Journalism, volume 2, no. 1 (February 2014) pp. 62–76

Chapter 6
The Use of Information and Communication Technologies in Three Egyptian Newsrooms
Ahmed El Gody
Digital Journalism, volume 2, no. 1 (February 2014) pp. 77–97

Chapter 7
Journalists' Twitter Networks, Public Debates and Relationships in South Africa
Peter Verweij and Elvira van Noort
Digital Journalism, volume 2, no. 1 (February 2014) pp. 98–114

Please direct any queries you may have about the citations to
clsuk.permissions@cengage.com

Notes on Contributors

Tanja Bosch, Centre for Film and Media Studies, University of Cape Town, South Africa

Ahmed El Gody, Media and Communication Studies, Örebro University, Sweden

Hayes Mawindi Mabweazara, School of Writing and Journalism, Falmouth University, UK

Admire Mare, School of Journalism and Media Studies, Rhodes University, South Africa

Motilola Olufenwa Akinfemisoye, School of Journalism and Digital Communication, University of Central Lancashire, UK

Elvira van Noort, EvN Media, Utrecht, The Netherlands

Peter Verweij, D3 Media, Arnhem, The Netherlands

For Tanaka and Nyasha

PREFACE

I am delighted to write a brief editorial note to introduce this special issue of *Digital Journalism* which focuses on the impact of new media technologies on African journalism, a focus which Guest Editor, Hayes Mawindi Mabweazara, notes is "scarce". The application of digital technologies to the traditional practice of journalism is reshaping every aspect of the production, content and reception of news and the newsrooms where it is produced. But the impact on journalism is distinctive in particular national settings, reflecting unique journalistic organisations, professional cultures, histories and economic resources. Consequently, understanding the relationship between new media technologies and a changing journalism practice requires an interpretive sensitivity to these particular socio-cultural and historical complexities. What is required, as Mabweazara notes, is "detailed qualitative explorations of how newsrooms (and their journalists) are adjusting to the new digital context of practice, as well as an understanding of the structure of the ensuing transformations from an African perspective".

The various research studies published here derive from five national settings and explore: the integration of digital technologies and mobile devices by free community newspaper *@Verdade* (Mozambique); the uses of social media at three community radio stations (South Africa); readers' responses to online news in state-controlled and private newspapers (Zimbabwe); the impact of user-generated content on election reporting in 2011 (Nigeria); and the implications of online technologies for journalism practice in three case study settings in private and state-controlled newspaper newsrooms (Egypt). The ambition is that these studies will assist in refashioning and de-Westernising accounts of African journalism. In the Guest Editor's words, this special issue should contribute towards "a reconstituted vision of global journalism practice in the digital era—one that validates the value of experiences outside Western countries ... but also demonstrates how new digital technologies have the potential to ... position African journalism in the unfolding global Information Society".

I am very grateful to Dr Hayes Mawinda Mabweazara for organising, editing and contributing to this collection of studies of journalism in Africa. Thanks also to each of the individual authors, the many anonymous reviewers of individual papers but especially to Herman Wasserman, Professor of Media and Deputy Head of School at Rhodes University, Grahamstown, South Africa, who read and commented on earlier drafts of all the papers which are published here.

Bob Franklin
Editor

INTRODUCTION

'Digital technologies and the evolving African newsroom': towards an African digital journalism epistemology

Hayes Mawindi Mabweazara

Introduction

Research into the impact of new digital technologies on African journalism is scarce. In particular, very little is known about the influence of digitisation, the internet, mobile communications and social media on the daily routines and practices of journalists in their "natural habitat"—*the newsroom* (Paterson and Domingo 2008). This gap in empirical research has often resulted in scholarly conjectures that, among other things, seek explanatory frameworks in the uneven distribution and use of technological resources between the economically developed North and the poor South. The resulting discourses invoke the "digital divide" as the default explanatory framework—seen by many as a chasm that prevents journalists in Africa from "drinking at the fount" (Berger 2005) of the unfolding digital revolution. Thus, African journalism is seen as being "in deficit as regards the emerging global information order" (Berger 2005, 1). The dominant discourse, as Berger further contends, is that "some of us have arrived in the land of plenty; the rest lag behind, empty-handed and hopeless, and urgently need to play catch-up or even leapfrog" (2). In short, "when seen in comparison with the First World, there are indeed shortcomings and a dire need for catch-up in [Africa]" (1). While this sense of backwardness aptly relates to setbacks associated with the realities of "access" to digital technologies, it also connects to the complexities and contradictions connected to the "localised" diffusion and permeation of digital technologies in African newsrooms. Collectively, these challenges, as Berger argues, inform much thinking about Africa in the global "Information Society", and often project an image of helpless journalists, who operate in conditions well below the purported level of their colleagues in the global North.

Yet, despite these challenges and prevailing assumptions, there is no denying the fact that African newsrooms (as elsewhere) are experiencing the disruptive—somewhat cataclysmic—impact of new digital technologies on the way news is generated, disseminated and consumed by their audiences. There are clear indications that a number of countries on the continent have functioning new technology facilities and indeed dimensions of internal newsroom creativity and adaptations to the digital revolution (however small) are emerging (see Accone 2000; Chari 2009; Berger 2011; Mabweazara 2011; Mudhai 2011; Mabweazara, Mudhai, and Whittaker 2014). Digital technologies are changing the informational needs of citizens and newsrooms (alongside their journalists) are being forced to adapt in various ways. As Berger (2005, 1) puts it: African journalists are "far from being mired in 'backwardness' or passively awaiting external salvation in regard to attempts to use [digital technologies]. Nor are they lacking when it comes to critical perspectives [towards the technologies]". Accone (2000, 69) similarly submits that despite challenges, "African journalists should hardly be viewed as second class Netizens. They have moulded Internet tools to suit their specific needs, devised ingenious technical solutions to overcome the idiosyncrasies of their situations, and continue to apply the medium [effectively in various contexts]". Nyamnjoh (2005, 4) concurs, arguing that African journalists are determined to be part of the technological revolutions of the modern world and "the way forward is in recognising the creative ways in which [they] merge their traditions with exogenous influences to create realities that are not reducible to either but enriched by both".

While efforts at assessing the changes spawned by the influence of new digital technologies are emerging, as noted above, a number of the studies tend to extrapolate "the experiences of a limited range of countries and regions to assume universal relevance" (Wasserman 2010, 10). What is particularly lacking are detailed qualitative explorations of how newsrooms (and their journalists) are adjusting to the new digital context of practice, as well as an understanding of the structure of the ensuing transformations from an African perspective. As Obonyo (2011, 1), rightly advises us, "there are unique peculiarities that demand that Africa isolates what is relevant and place it in Africa's unique situations, and weave out of that mosaic a framework that reflects Africa's reality". We, therefore, need to confront questions about whether "African circumstances and contexts provide new … insights that can extend the broad body of knowledge" (du Plessis 2012, 123) about journalism in "the digital era". In addition to this, we need to examine how those African circumstances and situations provide sufficient ground for the development of uniquely African experiences and perspectives on the impact of digital technologies on traditional journalism.

Towards an African Digital Journalism Epistemology

The research gap noted above has resulted in sustained dependence on Western theoretical and empirical constructs, which, in many cases, have little or no correspondence to the concrete and material realities of African journalists (Atton and Mabweazara 2011; Mabweazara et al. 2014). Most African journalists, as Paterson (2014, 259–260, emphasis added) observes, operate in multifaceted conditions "where news production is sometimes strikingly similar to what might be seen in any global news hub … and, conversely, *sometimes distant from Northern norms in terms of its goals and methods*". In the same way, as Kupe (2004) further notes, most African journalists work with significantly fewer resources. They have a lower status, are poorly paid and operate in multicultural countries that are at various stages of constituting themselves as nations in a globalising world. These contextual complexities and contradictions tend to be overlooked, consequently resulting in superficial and considerably anachronistic articulations of what developments in digital technologies actually mean for the practice of traditional journalism on the continent. This, as Ibelema (2008, 36) contends, has meant that professional norms and practices that emerge from Western social "processes are applied out of context, sometimes awkwardly" in the African context. Yet, even when "[t]heories and empirical studies developed in the West might appear to be applicable to the African context, … a closer look shows significant differences requiring nuanced theorising and research" (Atton and Mabweazara 2011, 668), especially given that much of the research is "conducted in splendid oblivion of conditions in [Africa]" (Berger 2000, 90). The studies have "evolved without incorporating the realities of Africa" (Obonyo 2011, 1) and hence covering only a small portion of the problems and situations that face African journalism. It is in this context that Nyamnjoh (1999, 15) avers that African journalism research must be located "in African realities and not in Western fantasies".

What we, therefore, need in addressing the research lacuna noted above, is a contextually rooted conceptual approach that enables us to maintain sensitivity to the unique professional and social dynamics in which African journalists operate. Thus, in exploring how African newsgatherers are adapting to the "vagaries" of the digital revolution, "we must acknowledge the complexity of the social context of news production and [avoid] the reductionistic idea of fixing news-making at one point along a circuit of interactions" (Mabweazara 2010, 22). In this sense, this special issue seeks to inspire and demonstrate sensitivity to the contingent nature of the interface between new digital technologies and traditional journalism practice in Africa by countering "technicist" approaches, which tend to extricate technologies from the social context of their deployment. As Conboy (2013, 149) reminds us, "Technology, in isolation, has never made journalism better or worse … [It] does not drive change. It has to adapt to the patterns of cultural expectation within particular societies at specific moments in time".

Accordingly, in examining how African newsrooms are adapting to the digital era, we should acknowledge the fact that technology by itself is not a relevant explanatory variable of emerging practices. Rather, we need to recognise both the rapidly changing technological aspects as well as the complex set of interactions between new technological possibilities and established journalistic forms. Thus, "[a]n assessment of journalism and technology needs insight from both the practice of journalism *as well as well as a general awareness of broader cultural trends and how technology forms part of social history*" (Conboy 2013, 149, emphasis added). In the same vein, the adoption and deployment of new digital technologies should be viewed as part of a complex social and institutional matrix, which stretches across a wide range of social institutions. The lines separating different technologies from one another and from society should thus be seen as relative and contingent upon a prevailing social consensus (Marx 1997).

This "calls for non-reductionist approaches that are sensitive to the complex interplay between multiple elements" (Mabweazara 2010, 22) at play in the everyday context in which new digital technologies are used in African newsrooms. Therefore, in seeking to understand how African journalists are adapting to the new digital era, we should not overlook the varied contextual influences—social, cultural, political and economic factors—"which lie outside journalism itself and indeed outside of any absolute consideration of the quality of journalism's products" (Conboy 2013, 149). All of these factors will help to shape and constrain the appropriations of new digital technologies. This line of thought relates to consistent calls to "de-Westernise" African media and communications research by examining and recognising the creative ways in which African journalists seek to harness, within the limits of pervasive "structural constraints

..., whatever possibilities are available to contest and seek inclusion" in the digital era (Nyamnjoh in Wasserman 2009, 291).

While a number of leading scholars have called for radical Afrocentric approaches to de-Westernising journalism studies (see Kasoma 1996), this themed issue is informed by a moderate heuristic approach that emphasises foregrounding the realities or contexts in which African journalists operate. To use Ngomba's (2012, 166) words, the issue "circumnavigates" radical Afrocentric discourses of de-Westernisation by accommodating (and in some cases modifying) Western theoretical approaches in ways that offer "contextually relevant extensions of [the] theories" to help frame our understanding of the impact of new digital technologies on traditional journalism in contemporary Africa. This approach leads to alternative understandings that foreground "localised" factors rooted in the antithesis of technological determinism—the social constructivist approach to technology. At the heart of this alternative perspective is sensitivity to the complex multi-dimensionality of elements of determinism (Dahlberg 2004) by paying attention to the "cultural and relational milieu" (Hays 1994, 66) (the deeper social, cultural, political and economic factors) at play in the deployment and appropriation of new technologies by African journalists.

This conceptual posture acknowledges the fact that the uses of technology take place in socially structured contexts, and as Thompson (1988, 368, emphasis added) reminds us, the first phase of cultural analysis should strive to "*reconstruct [the] context* and examine the social relations and institutions, the distribution of power and resources, by virtue of which this context forms a social field". Thus, in seeking answers to the impact of digital technologies on African newsroom, we need to look at African journalism in context—its culture, institutions, the broader communication environment—and examine how these collectively provide insights that can enable us to develop what we might loosely brand as an *African digital journalism epistemology*. This stance "allows us to view the use of new digital technologies by journalists as a multifaceted experience that can be evaluated against the backdrop of the local ... factors" (Mabweazara 2010, 25). As Obieng-Quaidoo (1986) contends, socio-cultural, political and economic aspects are central to any attempt to understand African journalism. With this awareness in mind, we can critically examine how new digital technologies are transforming newsmaking practices, and the ways in which they are being incorporated into the everyday lives of journalists, which inadvertently mediate the processes of adoption and use of new technologies. This sensitivity to *context* further helps to define African journalism in the digital era as well as position it in "the universals that are deaf-and-dumb to the particularities of journalism in and on Africa" (Nyamnjoh in Wasserman 2009, 287).

It is, however, important to highlight that while the emphasis on context is key here, Africa as a continent is not a homogenous landscape with a collective singular identity. It is, in fact, "a culturally, politically and economically ... fragmented society ... There are many Africans, *both fitting stereotyping but simultaneously defying uniform description*" (Obonyo 2011, 4, emphasis added). As Obonyo further contends, North Africa is more closely aligned to the Middle East than to the wider Africa. "It engages less in scholarship terms with the rest of the continent" (2). Consequently, conversations about Africa invariably consider Africa south of the Sahara. But even here disparities informed by "language and colonial experiences make it somewhat of a challenge to make sweeping statements" (2). There are wide discrepancies between Francophone,

Anglophone and Lusophone Africa and indeed within each of these regions. For example, South Africa stands apart from the rest of English-speaking Africa; its "media infrastructure is [predominantly well-funded, with excellent newsroom infrastructure hence] markedly different from the rest of the continent" (2).

In proposing the approach articulated above, as argued elsewhere, I am not "suggesting a localised research agenda of separatism" (Atton and Mabweazara 2011, 670), or falling into the "seductive perils of 'essentialism and ahistoricism'" that have characterised a number of non-Western alternative theoretical discussions in journalism and media research, rather the premise is that "where 'Western' theories appear relevant and promising … African scholars should neither shy away from using them, nor be apologetic when using them critically" (Ngomba 2012, 177), even as we seek to de-westernise our scholarly accounts and map out an *African digital journalism epistemology*.

About this Special Issue

Against the foregoing backdrop, this themed issue offers space to scholarship that interrogates and examines closely how African journalists are forging new ways of practising journalism in the context of technological changes in their newsrooms as well as in the wider context of news production. The issue is motivated by Cottle's instruction that with the rapid changes in the context in which journalism is practised, "we need to examine the fast changing ecology of news, its changing industrialised and technological basis and its response to the changing structurations of society" (Cottle 2000, 432). In this light, the six contributions to this issue detail trends, practices and emerging cultures of the adoption and appropriation of new digital technologies by newsrooms and journalists drawn from three African regions (North, West and Southern Africa), constituted by case studies selected from five countries: Egypt, Mozambique, South Africa, Nigeria and Zimbabwe. As highlighted above, the collection of essays is an attempt to offer "fresh" non-Western empirical insights into how traditional journalism is adapting to the unsettling impact of new digital technologies in their various forms. The issue broadly explores the diverse ways in which African newsrooms adopt and utilise new digital technologies in respect of their work, including the challenges and normative dilemmas emerging with the adoption of the technologies.

While the contributions to the issue are predominantly anchored in Western journalism theory they, however, point to a number of localised dimensions of appropriations of new technologies as defined by the socio-political structures in which journalists (and their newsrooms) operate. In particular, the essays demonstrate the possibilities for uniquely African views that enrich our understanding of *adoption practices, localised appropriations* as well as cultures emerging with *interactivity and networking*. The studies further demonstrate, as noted earlier, that even within particular regions on the African continent, including individual countries, newsrooms' adoption of new digital technologies are enormously varied and far from being homogenous. This reinforces a point made earlier that Africa *is not a singular entity*; rather it has nuances and differences that often evade the purview of researchers steeped in Western journalism scholarship.

The essays published here largely deploy qualitative research approaches that offer rich observation and descriptions that challenge popular assumptions about the impact of new digital technologies on African journalism. With the research widely dominated by Anglophone cases, Admire Mare shifts our focus to a unique setting, Mozambique (a Lusophone country), where the media landscape is predominantly under-researched. He offers a thoughtful discussion of the creative appropriation and innovative integration of new digital technologies, including mobile channels by a community newspaper, *@Verdade* that circulates free of charge. The study makes reference to "local context" appropriations of Facebook, as well as its "symbolic" recreation in the physical space through writing and illustrating breaking news in formats that demonstrate the creative rearticulating of technology to fit into deprived African contexts in line with local needs and expectations. The notion of the "digital divide" is thus at the core of the study, in particular, how questions of "access" to technology (in its various forms) shape and constrain the news-agenda of local newspapers. This further relates to language complexities, especially the dominance of English language as a medium of engagement on the internet (at the expense of local languages), and the consequent implications on wider "access".

In contrast to the print-first or text-based approaches to journalism considered by most of the contributors to this special issue, Tanja Bosch concentrates on converging technologies and practices in South African community radio journalism. Focusing on radio stations in three major cities, she addresses how social media is deployed and the implications for the notion of "community radio" when stations migrate to digital spaces. While emphasising the fact that South African community radio journalism is not homogenous because of various factors, including location, funding and skills levels, Bosch observes that the community radio stations use digital technologies to connect with their audiences. The radio stations no longer see their audiences in the traditional sense, in which they are organised around *identity politics* or *communal social relations*, but rather as "atomised" individuals who connect with the stations increasingly via digital platforms which have become extensions of the airwaves, consequently stretching the boundaries of traditional "community radio". However, the pervasive nature of the "digital divide" has not spared the radio stations as the bulk of their audience is constituted by low-income groups with limited access to the internet or mobile phones. The inequalities of access to digital technologies highlighted in this study point to South Africa's social dilemma which is marked by a yawning chasm between the rich and the poor. Thus, while digital technologies have become central to the daily routines of community radio stations, they have in essence not radically transformed the radio stations' approaches to their journalism.

While acknowledging that journalists have not always capitalised upon the creative ways in which the public they target adopt, adapt and appropriate new technologies, Hayes Mawindi Mabweazara extends Mare and Bosch's discussion in his examination of how readers' responses to the interactivity of online news content have become central to news cultures and practices in Zimbabwe's state-controlled and private press. Mabweazara explores the intersections between audience voices and traditional journalism, and argues that readers' comments are increasingly shaping and contributing to the dynamics of newsmaking in ways that point to a reconfiguration of the traditional news culture. Further, the comment forums also provide alternative spaces for public deliberation, a key function in a context where general information flows and censorship of the media by government are rife. However, for Mabweazara, the integration of user comments in this heavily polarised journalistic context is not without negative implications. In particular, the lack of clear and consistent gatekeeping strategies has opened floodgates of abuses and extremist views that pose serious social threats as well as taint the core values and normative ideals of news. Motilola Olufenwa Akinfemisoye's study similarly focuses on the impact of "alternative user voices" (mediated by new technologies) on Nigerian mainstream newsroom culture in the context of the 2011 general election. She argues that in the context of the election, Nigerian newsrooms sought to maximise profits by actively engaging "alternative audience voices" in reporting the elections. However, while the adoption of user-generated content (UGC) in mainstream news reporting is challenging and recasting established institutional practices and cultures, it is not necessarily redefining the traditional journalistic structure. Akinfemisoye concludes that contrary to scholarship that sees digital technologies as "de-professionalising" journalists, mainstream journalism in Nigeria makes every effort to defend its territory by going beyond just breaking news to providing more in-depth and interpretive reports.

With an emphasis on new technology *adoption* and *innovation* in Egyptian print newsrooms, Ahmed El Gody offers a detailed account of how new technologies are influencing newsroom practices. Focusing on three case studies drawn from the state-controlled and private press, El Gody highlights how organisational approaches, attitudes, as well as internal "power dynamics" shape and constrain the adoption, access and use of new technologies by journalists. Adopting a detailed descriptive approach, the study demonstrates how local context factors, including proprietorial influences and management attitudes, shape adoption practices in African newsrooms. El Gody concludes that ownership patterns and variations between types of news organisations influence the adoption and appropriation of new technologies. Thus, while the pro-government press seem far from understanding the centrality of new technologies as journalistic tools, the "independent" private press has invested heavily in the technologies and innovatively deploys them to escape government control as well as to connect and interact with sources and audiences.

Peter Verweij and Elvira van Noort remind us how the South African journalism context has more in common with the Western media context than with the broader sub-Saharan Africa in their examination of how social media (Twitter, specifically) is deployed by a network of journalists to connect with various stakeholders in the news-making culture. They observe that the South African journalists' "Twitter network" is characterised by pluralism; with a number of journalists from leading mainstream newsrooms, as well as freelance journalists, taking the lead as influential voices on Twitter. Verweij and van Noort argue that journalists' role in the network is not just limited to searching for story ideas and disseminating news, but also extends to commenting on stories as well as inviting the public to actively take part in topical discussions. In this sense, Twitter as a "journalistic network" strengthens the independence of public debate in a context where the government is bent on controlling information flows. In the same way, the openness and pluralism expressed by various subgroups in the network is key to shaping public debate and engendering democratic decision-making.

Although the picture painted in these studies is not an unequivocally rosy one, with some of the case studies clearly demonstrating that much work still needs to be done in embracing "convergence practices" in African newsrooms, the papers, nonetheless, illustrate the agency and creativity displayed by journalists (and their newsrooms) in adopting and adapting digital technologies to their specific contexts. Collectively, the studies make a "compelling case for delving into the lived materialities of reportorial forms, practices and epistemologies, showing us wherein lie the challenges, as well as the remarkable potentials" (Allan 2014, x), for African journalism as it evolves across multiple digital platforms.

Further, while the studies highlight the significance of *locale*, they are not confined to Africa, they are in dialogue with mainstream theoretical concerns that originate elsewhere, hence pointing to the significance of cross-cultural comparative studies that "reconnect accounts of journalism in Africa with Western research" (Atton and Mabweazara 2011, 670). Taken together, the papers not only showcase alternative ways of understanding and explaining issues at the heart of the changing nature of traditional journalism, but also highlight the centrality of the fact that "No theorisation takes place in a void. Meaningful theorisation has to be contextualised" (Nyamnjoh in Wasserman 2009, 283). Thus, even as we seek to de-westernise our accounts by deploying an African digital journalism epistemology, we do not necessarily need to substitute or replace existing theory as "The African condition is not a birthmark; it is not exclusive to Africa" (287).

It is hoped that these accounts will contribute towards a reconstituted vision of global journalism practice in the digital era—one that not only validates the value of experiences outside Western countries (particularly the United Kingdom and the United States), but also demonstrates how new digital technologies have the potential to boost "African stories, information, and representations for African audiences" (Berger 2005, 1), thereby positioning African journalism in the unfolding global Information Society.

It is worth noting, however, that a cogent realisation of the theoretical posture advanced above is beyond the boundaries of the research covered here. The special issue is far from providing an exhaustive picture of the intersections between digital technologies and journalism practice in Africa. Rather, it provides an empirical point of departure for further scholarly explorations that mainstream African perspectives into current debates about the impact of new technologies on journalism. In particular, there is scope for further research that shifts focus from the country-specific case studies presented here to broader comparative investigations that examine developments between African countries as well as other regions of the global South. This, however, does not imply simply expanding on the regions covered by this issue, but also entails deploying the emerging evidence to critically engage with the dominant Western theoretical constructs, which are so heavily relied upon by researchers, not least the contributors to this themed issue.

REFERENCES

Accone, Tanya. 2000. "Digital Dividends for Journalism in Africa." *Nieman Reports.* 54 (4): 67–69.

Allan, Stuart. 2014. "Foreword." In *Online Journalism in Africa: Trends, Practices and Emerging Cultures*, edited by Mabweazara, Hayes M., Mudhai, Okoth F. and Whittaker, Jason, ix–x. London: Routledge.

Atton, Chris, and Mabweazara, Hayes M. 2011. "New Media and Journalism Practice in Africa: An Agenda for Research." *Journalism: Theory, Practice & Criticism* 12 (6): 667–673.

Berger, Guy. 2000. "Grave New World? Democratic Journalism Enters the Global Twenty-First Century." *Journalism Studies* 1 (1): 81–99.

Berger, Guy. 2005. "Powering African Newsrooms: Theorising How Southern African Journalists Make Use of ICTs for Newsgathering." In *Doing Digital Journalism: How Southern African Newsgatherers Are Using ICTs*, edited by Guy. Berger, 1–14. Grahamstown: High Way Africa.

Berger, Guy. 2011. "Empowering the Youth as Citizen Journalists: A South African Experience." *Journalism: Theory, Practice & Criticism* 12 (6): 708–726.

Chari, Tendai. 2009. "Ethical Challenges Facing Zimbabwean Media in the Context of the Internet." *Global Media Journal: African Edition* 3 (1): 1–34.

Conboy, Martin. 2013. *Journalism Studies: The Basics*. London: Routledge.

Cottle, Simon. 2000. "Rethinking News Access." *Journalism Studies*. 1 (3): 427–448.

Dahlberg, Lincoln. 2004. "Internet Research Tracings: Towards Non-Reductionist Methodology." *Journal of Computer Mediated Communication* 9 (3). Accessed June 14, 2006. http://jcmc.indiana.edu/vol9/issue3/dahlberg.html

du Plessis, Danie. 2012. "Introduction: African Communication/Media Theory." *Communicatio* 38 (2): 123–126.

Hays, Sharon. 1994. "Structure and Agency and the Sticky Problem of Culture." *Sociological Theory* 12 (1): 57–72.

Ibelema, Minabere. 2008. *The African Press, Civic Cynicism, and Democracy*. New York: Pelgrave Mcmillan.

Kasoma, Francis. 1996. "The Foundations of African Ethics (Afri-Ethics) and the Professional Practice of Journalism: The Case for Society-Centred Media Morality." *African Media Review* 10 (3): 93–116.

Kupe, Tawana. 2004. "An Agenda for Researching African Media and Communication Contexts." *Ecquid Novi: South African Journal for Journalism Research* 25 (2): 353–356.

Mabweazara, Hayes M. 2010. "'New' Technologies and Journalism Practice in Africa: Towards a Critical Sociological Approach." In *The Citizen in Communication: Re-Visiting Traditional, New and Community Media Practices in South Africa*, edited by Nathalie Hyde-Clarke, 11–30. Capetown: Juta & Co.

Mabweazara, Hayes M. 2011. "The Internet in the Print Newsroom: Trends, Practices and Emerging Cultures in Zimbabwe." In *Making Online News Newsroom Ethnographies in the Second Decade of Internet Journalism*, edited by David Domingo and Chris Paterson, 57–69. New York: Peter Lang.

Mabweazara, Hayes M., Okoth F. Mudhai, and Whittaker, Jason, eds. 2014. *Online Journalism in Africa: Trends, Practices and Emerging Cultures Mabweazara*. London: Routledge.

Marx, Leo. 1997. "Technology: The Emergence of a Hazardous Concept." *Social Research* 64 (3): 965–988.

Mudhai, Okoth F. 2011. "Immediacy and Openness in a Digital Africa: Networked-Convergent Journalisms in Kenya." *Journalism: Theory, Practice and Criticism* 12 (6): 674–691.

Ngomba, Teke. 2012. "Circumnavigating De-Westernisation: Theoretical Reflexivities in Researching Political Communication in Africa." *Communicatio* 38 (2): 164–180.

Nyamnjoh, Francis. B. 1999. "African Cultural Studies, Cultural Studies in Africa: How to Make a Useful Difference." *Critical Arts: A Journal of Cultural Studies in Africa* 13 (1): 15–39.

Nyamnjoh, Francis. B. 2005. *Africa's Media: Democracy and the Politics of Belonging*. London: Zed Books.

Obeng-Quaidoo, Isaac. 1986. "A Proposal for New Communication Research Methodologies in Africa." *Africa Media Review* 1 (1): 89–98.

Obonyo, Levi. 2011. "Towards a Theory of Communication for Africa: The Challenges for Emerging Democracies." *Communicatio* 37 (1): 1–20.

Paterson, Chris. 2014. "Epilogue." In *Online Journalism in Africa Trends, Practices and Emerging Cultures*, edited by Mabweazara, Hayes M., Mudhai, Okoth F. and Whittaker, Jason, 259–261. London: Routledge.

Paterson, Chris, and Domingo, David, eds. 2008. *Making Online News: An Ethnography of New Media Production*, 1–11. New York: Peter Lang.

Thompson, John B. 1988. "Mass Communication and Modern Culture: Contribution to a Critical Theory of Ideology." *Sociology*. 22 (3): 359–383.

Wasserman, Herman. 2009. "Extending the Theoretical Cloth to Make Room for African Experience." *Journalism Studies* 10 (2): 281–293.

Wasserman, Herman, ed. 2010. *Popular Media, Democracy and Development in Africa*. London: Routledge.

NEW MEDIA TECHNOLOGIES AND INTERNAL NEWSROOM CREATIVITY IN MOZAMBIQUE

The case of *@verdade*

Admire Mare

This paper discusses the various ways in which a community newspaper in Mozambique is creatively appropriating new media technologies to enhance its news production and distribution practices. Far from being backward, the case of @Verdade demonstrates that despite being under-resourced, community newspapers in Africa are catching up in terms of creatively appropriating new media technologies. Besides spawning new ways of practising journalism, this article argues that the pervasiveness of new media technologies in the routines of the @Verdade *newsroom has engendered collaborative storytelling while at the same time destabilizing traditional journalism's ethical practices. Using data drawn from qualitative research, the study discusses how the use of social network sites, the mobile phone as well as the internet in general are aiding @Verdade to generate and engage with news sources as well as deliver content to diverse audiences. Drawing on structuration theory (as modified by Orlikowski) and the sociology of journalism approach, the paper argues that the disruptive impact of new media technologies needs to be understood as a duality of influences—the human agency of individual journalists and owners (internal newsroom creativity)* vis-à-vis *the wider context of news production (restructuring of journalism practice).*

Introduction

Despite the fact that Africa is the least connected continent on the internet (only 15.6 per cent penetration rate[1]), the use of information and communication technologies (ICTs) is becoming pervasive and deeply embedded in journalistic routines and cultures (Obijiofor 2003).Thus the introduction of new media technologies has raised questions about the extent to which existing media work will change as a result. Accompanying the digital revolution has been radical shifts in journalism which have changed every aspect of the production, content and reception of news (Obijiofor 2003). In some contexts, journalism has metamorphosed from a lecture format into a conversation (dialogical, participatory, collaborative, interactive storytelling). Besides spawning ubiquitous news, the changes are associated with increased global access to information, instantaneous reporting, interactivity, multimedia content and extreme customization. They have also revised the "circuit of culture" (du Gay et al. 1997) by allowing erstwhile readers to become active participants in the creation and dissemination of news and information. At the structural level, new media technologies have altered routines both within newsrooms and out in the field. These crucial changes challenge traditional assumptions in journalism practice, scholarship and education. They make definitional boundaries fluid and call for a reassessment of even the most fundamental questions such as "What is journalism?", "What is news?", "What is the difference between news and information?" and "Who is a journalist?"

A number of studies have been conducted on the impact of new media technologies on journalism practice in African countries (Moyo 2009; Atton and Mabweazara 2011; Mabweazara 2011; Jordan 2013; Mare 2013; Paterson and Doctors 2013). Participatory journalism, in which narrowly defined "social media" practices such as blogging, tweeting and Facebook play an integral role, is thriving around Africa (Paterson and Doctors 2013). Most of the early researches on the impact of new media technologies have focused on the "interactive" features of online editions of African newspapers (Obijiofor 2003; Berger 2005). Interactive features are hailed for allowing users to comment, give feedback or even vote on controversial issues. In a study conducted by Obijiofor (2003, 54) in Ghana and Nigeria, it was found that "new media technologies are helping journalists to save time in their work as well as improving the quality of newspapers by accelerated speed of production, enhancement of newspaper aesthetics and ease of crosschecking spelling errors with the aid of the spell check software". Writing on how Southern African journalists deploy new media technologies, Berger (2005, 1) points out that the journalists "are far from being mired in 'backwardness' or passively awaiting external salvation in regard to attempts to use ICTs". For him, despite contextual factors peculiar to Africa, journalists are actively deploying new technologies in their professional functions. In the case of mobile technology, Mabweazara (2011, 693) argues that it has decentred the arena of news making in Zimbabwe's mainstream press by offering an alternative avenue for news gathering and dissemination within the state-controlled and the private press. In South Africa, the "quality" press has been at the forefront of adapting to international trends in convergence and interactivity "in an attempt to halt declining circulation figures" (Wasserman 2010, 20). Despite the mediating role of new media technologies, most of these studies show that the physical space and face-to-face meetings remain essential and under-gird journalists' professional practice.

In recent years, research on the impact of new media technologies has shifted towards the study of citizen journalism practices. Within this strand of research, the mobile phone is seen as being leveraged to varying degrees by citizens to contribute to news making. Thus ordinary citizens armed with mobile phones and other media tools are able to capture "news" in real or close-to-real time—much more immediately and rapidly than professional journalists. Citizen journalism has also contributed a great deal to the circulation of public opinion, and has to some extent influenced the way mainstream media cover important events such as elections (see Moyo 2009). Focusing on the relationship between social media and mainstream media in the coverage of Southern African protests, Mare (2013, 83) argues that while social media were instrumental in breaking news during social protests, mainstream media weighed in with verification, contextualization and amplification. The point here is that despite their initial misgivings about the credibility of the information disseminated via digital technologies, mainstream journalists worldwide have gradually started to adopt social media as professional tools (Jordan 2013).

But despite the aforementioned burgeoning literature focusing on the impact of new media technologies on African newsrooms, little is known about how Mozambican newspapers are coping with the compelling pressures associated with the digital revolution. As Atton and Mabweazara (2011, 668) observe, "research has largely lacked theoretical and empirical grounding in terms of examining how African mainstream journalists are forging 'new' ways to practice their profession in light of technological changes in their newsrooms". While drawing on theoretical debates extrapolated from "media-saturated societies", this study endeavours to explore how new media technologies are being creatively appropriated by *@Verdade* in Mozambique. Moreover, very little attention has been paid to new media technologies as "tools" for news production in mainstream journalism practice (Mabweazara 2010). A clarion call has also been made on the need for ethnographic newsroom studies to improve the understanding of the complex interactions between changing news technologies and journalist practices (Jordan 2013). This study therefore seeks to fill a lacuna on unique, different and contingent appropriations of new media technologies and emerging newsroom cultures in the Mozambican context.

New Media Technologies and Journalism: The Great Debate?

Bearing in mind the polarised nature of the never-ending debate on the meaning of the term "new" media technologies, this paper uses the phrase loosely to refer to the internet, interactive websites, the mobile phone, social network sites (Facebook, Twitter and YouTube, etc.), mobile instant messaging (Mxit, Whatsapp, etc.) and other digital telecommunications. Although the advent of new media technologies in Africa in the 1990s "sparked celebratory, almost utopian bliss" (Banda, Mudhai, and Wisdom 2009, 1), one of its offspring, citizen journalism, has met with strong opposition and criticism from media commentators (Fenton 2010; Saleh 2010). For Hermida (2011), the emergence of online tools that allow for broad participation in the creation and dissemination of content has repercussions for the role of journalists as conveyors of news and information. In Europe and America, "prophets of doom" have announced the imminent death of journalism, while others have already composed funeral dirges such as the infamous "Long live journalism, print is eternal".[2] Much of the public debate on the relationship between new media technologies and journalism has taken place within the blogosphere, perhaps reflecting the slow pace of academic publishing. Anderson (2005) captures this cynicism as follows: "Faced with the challenge of analyzing the impact of the internet and its various journalistic stepchildren on traditional forms of news gathering and reporting, media commentators tend to adopt an unfortunate all-or-nothing rhetoric." McNair (2009, 347–348), however, reassuringly states: "Journalism will not die out in this environment, because it is needed on so many social, political and cultural levels. Journalism has a future." Most alarmist critiques of the perceived impact of new media technologies on journalism have fallen into the trap of technological determinism, which downplays the role of political, social and cultural factors in shaping ICT uses by journalists, and hence they suffer from a poverty of nuanced analysis. As McNair (2009, 347) insightfully observes, "the future of journalism is often conflated with the future of a particular journalistic medium, currently print". While newspapers are in crisis in advanced capitalist societies, it must be noted that circulation figures are expanding in India and other developing countries (McNair 2009).

The reaction of "moral panic" against citizen journalism (as against tabloids before that) is promoted by journalists and news organizations whose loud and strident voices warn of the growth of slacktivism (the act of participating in obviously pointless activities as an expedient alternative to actually expending effort to fix a problem) and noise within the communication ecosystem. For Hermida (2011), current academic debates on how new media technologies complement or compete against journalism often turn into legitimation battles about whether the "*de facto*" solution is a new media network rather than a media institution. Some scholars have framed the ongoing changes within journalism as amounting to a "crisis", while others see it as a boon for innovative newsrooms. Such debates serve to police the boundaries of the profession by reiterating accepted definitions of what it is to be a journalist. When these boundaries are transgressed, the paradigm is threatened (Wasserman 2005). In the words of Berger (2011, 708), "there has been both a celebration of outsider involvement in mass communications on the one side, where the fifth estate is seen as ameliorating the deficiencies in the media, and ending the monopolistic 'priesthood' of journalism and a defensive response at the other extreme". In terms of theoretical debates on the interplay between journalism and new media technologies, three broad categories are identifiable: (1) supporters who hail the democratic virtues of new media technologies; (2) detractors who critique new media technologies for creating problems for journalism; and (3) those who advocate a middle-ground approach to promote synergies between the "fourth" and the "fifth" estates.

Supporters of citizen journalism see it as an opportunity to "democratize" rather than "deprofessionalize" journalism. New media technologies are seen as a "goldmine" that presents journalists with new opportunities for improved practice (Berger 2005). New media technologies are also deemed to introduce a new dimension to journalism by allowing a space for contributions and opinions. They are credited with giving people an opportunity to voice their own thoughts and opinions—something traditional media platforms lack. Advocates of citizen journalism highlight its instrumental role during the Arab Spring (Newman 2011) and the 2008 elections in Zimbabwe (Moyo 2009). According to proponents of citizen journalism, interactive media applications clearly democratize representation by making it a more direct relationship: as citizens gain access to inexpensive communication technologies, the gatekeeping monopoly editors and broadcasters once enjoyed, is waning. New media technologies have revised the "circuit of culture" through the convergence of the production and the consumption of news. This occurs not merely through passive bespoke consumption, but through active engagement via blogging, re-posting, commenting, recommending, rating, tagging and the like. Far from cannibalizing news produced by the mainstream media, social media are helping media organizations to direct traffic to news sites.

Opponents of citizen journalism accuse it of assuming everyone who has access to digital technologies spontaneously becomes a "journalist". As Berger (2011, 709) writes, even "having access to media production facilities does not necessarily mean that people have the skills or desire to make use of these opportunities—for any kind of content output, let alone journalistic content". Instead of democratizing journalism, Fenton (2010) notes that such claims associated with digital technologies are grossly overstated. New media, she claims, have both enabled and accelerated shifts in journalistic practice that results in the homogenization of news content across competing outlets and multiple platforms; improper, sometimes outright unethical, sourcing of articles; a deterioration of working conditions for journalists; increasing reliance upon a few, trusted mainstream voices and forces on the periphery of the journalistic field (Fenton 2010). Linking the proliferation of new media technologies to neo-colonialism, Saleh (2010) argues that that technology is not politically neutral, but has been "imagined" in certain ways, and is inherently bound up with particular notions of ownership. She makes strong connections between the rise of the IT revolution and the advent of neoliberalism and globalization, demonstrating that citizens in core economies have very limited input into the internet governance process, whereas citizens from poor economies have almost no such input. New media technologies are also castigated for destabilising "tried and tested" business models through their promotion of "free online news". As Newman (2011, 10) argues, "social media are changing the production, distribution and discovery of news and further disrupting the business models of mainstream media companies". Facebook and Twitter stand accused of living parasitically off the quality content produced by mainstream media and reaping the commercial benefit. Even more scathing has been criticism voiced against the quality and reliability of information available on social media, along with the dumbing down of the agenda of information, while others point to new perspectives opening up (McNair 2009). There are fears that the filtering of news sources through friends and colleagues could minimize diversity and reinforce prejudices. According to Newman (2011), early debates focused on the credibility and reliability of social media and whether they would destroy "old media". Detractors regard new media technologies as an "invasive weed" with the power to "deprofessionalize" journalism. Journalism today finds itself at a rare moment in history where, for the first time, its hegemony as gatekeeper of the news is threatened not just by new technology and competitors but potentially, by the audience it serves. Newman (2011) describes the potentially conflictual relationship between social media and journalism as expression of a clash of style and cultures over the unregulated, anything-goes nature of the peer-to-peer internet. Despite these seemingly different epistemological roots, mainstream journalism and citizen journalism complement each other in a myriad of ways. For instance, broadcast news often feeds off and incorporates elements of citizen journalism through the use of eyewitness footage from mobile phones, the reporting of stories originally broken by citizen journalism initiatives on the Web, or even guest reporter slots in which citizens participate in packaging an item for a television or radio newscast.

A middle-ground perspective has been offered by a number of scholars who see the social media as fostering "collaborative reporting" (Hermida 2011), which reincarnates the notion of "public" or "civic" journalism. At the core of public journalism is the belief that "journalism has an obligation to public life—an obligation that goes beyond just telling the news or unloading lots of facts. The way we do our journalism affects the way public life goes. Journalism can help empower a community or it can help to disable it." To journalistic reformers, reporting has always been something of a collaborative process between journalists and their sources. Social media are hailed for opening the newsroom doors and demanding a conversation, not just a response. The internet and new media technologies are actually helping to achieve some of the core goals of journalism: strengthening society, communities and democracy, in part through sharing information.

The Research Context: Mozambican Media Landscape

Mozambique emerged from years of bitter civil war in 1992 and quickly revoked its Marxist socialist leanings by embracing neoliberal economic policies (Lloyd 2011). These policies set Mozambique on a trajectory of rapid economic growth, averaging about 7 per cent per year—although that growth has done little to improve the country's overall level of development. The country has won many admirers for its stable political and economic system, but its superficial stability and prosperity (for a few and for the politically well-connected) has masked widespread social and economic disparities that threaten what passes for peaceful rule (Jacobs and Duarte 2010). The country is beset by huge challenges, for instance, half of the adult population cannot read or write; more than 80 per cent do not have access to electricity; 55 per cent live in poverty, 12 per cent carry HIV, the virus that causes Aids, and corruption is rampant (Lloyd 2011). Discontent reached fever pitch in September 2010 when state-sanctioned rises in food and transport prices sparked social unrest in which at least 14 people were killed by the police. Although the government was able to deal with the situation, it was only the tip of the iceberg of public discontent fermenting in Mozambique.

Given the limited intellectual dialogue between Lusophone, Francophone and Anglophone Africa attributed to language differences, little is known about Mozambique's media landscape. Although media advocacy organisations exhort the country's media freedom, such glorification hides a very different reality in Mozambican journalism. For instance, the country is ranked 66 out of 179 countries listed in the Reporters Sans Frontières (RSF) 2011–12 World Press Freedom Index. The country also inherited destroyed infrastructure and severe poverty which means that many areas do not receive news and information on a regular basis (Lloyd 2011). Freedom of the press was guaranteed through the 1990 Constitution, while the first new democratic media law was passed a year later (Lloyd 2011). This paved the way for the launch of an independent daily newssheet, *Mediafax*, which was distributed via fax. Following the arrival of the internet in Mozambique, *Mediafax* switched to distribution by email. Other notable newspapers include *Savana, Noticias, O Pais, Diário de Moçambique, Canal de Moçambique* and *Canalmoz*. Public media such as Agencia da Informacao de Mocambique (AIM) and Televisao de Mocambique (TVM) represent some of the most blatant mouthpieces of the ruling party. It is notable to highlight that the country suffers from endemic high turnover of private newspapers attributable to high levels of illiteracy and structural poverty. High media mortality is also caused by the absence of advertising, labour turnover within newsrooms and lack of reading culture. It is within this harsh media environment that *@Verdade* emerged after identifying a gap in the market.

In terms of internet connectivity, Mozambique was the first African country to offer broadband wireless services through the Worldwide Interoperability for Microwave Access (WiMax).[3] The gradual liberalization of telecommunications in 2000 has been accompanied by notable improvements in the sector. Since the roll-out of SEACOM and the Eastern African Submarine Cable System (EASSY) submarine cables in July 2009 and July 2010, respectively, the backbone of the network has expanded tremendously.

Telecomunicaoes de Mocambique has been at the centre of modernizing the telecommunications infrastructure (Lloyd 2011). This state-driven initiative has seen all provincial capitals connected to the national grid via fibre broadband links. Despite reduced internet prices following the laying of fibre broadband links, most Mozambicans cannot afford to have individual connections, because the costs are too high compared with other countries in the region (a 1 megabit/second (Mbps) leased line/month costs US $4000 and 1 Mbps ADSL residential line/month costs US$175). In an attempt to reach universal service and access, the state has rolled out community access points in the form of internet cafes and Provincial Digital Resource Centres (CPRDs). These points are community owned and combine rural radio broadcasting, computers and access to the internet. By early 2012 about 20 CRPDs had been set up, mostly in the south of the country, although it is not clear which socio-economic groups make use of them. Other important access points have been established in schools, through the Schoolnet project, which implements computer rooms in schools, for training students in ICT basics. Mozambique had 7.7 million mobile subscribers at the end of 2011, according to the GSMA, an association of the world's main mobile networks and more than 20 internet service providers (www.infoasaid.org). The three mobile operators, Mcel, Vodacom and Movitel, also offer internet access using 3G, broadband and wireless. According to the Internet World Stats 2011 data, Mozambique has a comparatively low rate of internet penetration with only 4.3 per cent (amounting to 975,395 people) of the population having access to the internet, while 186,460 users (about 0.8 per cent) were on Facebook. These low internet figures are understandable because of the low levels of English literacy in the country. According to the 2007 census, about 50.4 per cent of all people aged 5 and older speak Portuguese and 10.7 per cent speak it as their first language. The more frequent mother tongue language is Makhuwa (26.3 per cent), followed by Changana (11.4 per cent) and Lomwe (7.9 per cent). English is widely spoken by the elite in government and business.

Theoretical and Methodological Approach

In order to make sense of the creative appropriation of new media technologies within a newsroom set up, this study draws on the "sociology of news production" and structuration theory (as revised by Orlikowski 1992). Both the "sociology of news production" approach and structuration theory provide a powerful conceptual resource which enables us to analyse the complex ways in which new media technologies interplay with the lived dynamics of journalists and the wider social context in which journalism is practised. The sociology of journalism has concerned itself with questions about what constitutes news, the (multi-dimensional) factors (political, economic, social organisational and cultural) that shape it and broadly argues that news is a social product shaped by the interactions among media professionals, media organisations and society (Manning 2001; Schudson 2005). As Mabweazara (2010, 11) aptly puts it, sociology of journalism's "emphasis on the 'institutional' and 'professional' factors to newsgathering places importance on the 'internal' workings of news production which have implications on how journalists deploy new technologies in their professional routines". An advantage of deploying the sociology of journalism is its insistence that there is need to understand the dialectical nature of news production and its relationship to the wider system of the news production processes. This chimes with structuration theory, which "refuse[s] to afford either technology or society a deterministic role, but view technology and society in interaction" (Wasserman 2011, 156; see also Orlikowski 1992). Propounded by British sociologist Anthony Giddens, it offers "an account of human agency which recognizes that human beings are purposive actors, who virtually all the time know what they are doing … and why" (Giddens 1984, 258). Giddens' theory has been modified by Orlikowski (1992, 409) to explain technology's duality and flexibility—duality in terms of technology being "constructed by actors working in a given social context". He also sees technology as being "socially constructed by actors through the different means they attach to it"—and flexibility with regards to the capacity of users to interpret, appropriate and manipulate technology in various ways (Orlikowski 1992, 409). Its basic premise is that technologies do not have effects built into them, because it is always a question of how particular technologies come to be institutionalized in particular ways.

In short, structuration theory attempts to move away from instrumental and technological deterministic methods, thereby privileging the mutual shaping of society and technology. Both theories enable us to straddle the bifurcation of structure and human agency in the interests of doing justice both to the agency of those who use new media technologies and the cultural, economic and social constraints which affect users (journalists). These approaches are relevant for us to critically analyse the complex questions of technology, agency and structure in the deployment of new media technologies in organizational settings.

Thus, both theoretical approaches converge in the sense that they acknowledge that journalists live and work within an encompassing social and cultural context that powerfully and implicitly informs their attempts to make sense of the world. In the context of the present study, theoretical convergences between the two provide a useful conceptual resource to analyse the unique, different and contingent appropriations of new media technologies and emerging newsroom cultures in the Mozambican context.

To gather data for the study, I deployed an ethnographic case-study approach that focused on one community newspaper based in Maputo, Mozambique.[4] I employed participant observation as an ethnographic approach in conjunction with in-depth (focus group and individual) interviews which provided context-specific perspectives of newsroom creativity and cultures in news production and distribution. This meant the researcher immersed himself in the newsroom culture firstly as an observer before taking up the role of naïve participant. Research participants were debriefed by the management on the purpose of the research while the researcher was introduced to the whole newsroom team. Beyond this routine debriefing session, the researcher requested informed consent from individual journalists and also assured them of confidentiality. The newsroom observation process lasted for two weeks (in January and February 2012). Focusing specifically on the daily activities of journalists, the researcher observed journalists using a wide range of technologies (including the mobile phone, telephones, the internet and social media platforms such as Whatsapp, Facebook and Twitter) during their day-to-day journalistic practices. Informal conversations were held with journalists who were fluent in English during the observation process. In-depth individuals and focus group discussions were also held during diary sessions and the end of the week parties which were held every Friday after work at the offices. The semi-structured interviews were preferred over structured interviews to allow for maximum flexibility and to make the respondents more at ease. As a naïve participant, the researcher also accompanied *@Verdade* staff during one of their newspaper distribution missions in Maputo. This enabled me to have first-hand information on how the newspaper distributes its free copies using motor bikes. During the fieldwork process, eight journalists (six males and two females) were interviewed at the *@Verdade* newsroom in Maputo. Because the research's aim was primarily to understand particulars rather than generalizing to universals, interviewees were recruited based on non-probability methods, including convenience and purposive sampling. Purposive sampling was very useful for this research because I needed to reach a targeted sample (journalists) in the shortest possible time and therefore sampling for proportionality was not the main concern. Whereas focus group and in-depth interviews were tape-recorded and transcribed, fieldwork notes were written during break and lunch sessions in order to avoid memory lapses.

The Digitally Converged Newsroom Environment: *@Verdade*

Launched in August 2008, *@Verdade* is the first and only community newspaper which is distributed for free in Mozambique. Started by an engineer-turned-corporate leader and social activist, Eric Charas (who contributed 80 per cent of the capital) and a few other business associates (the remaining 20 per cent), the weekly paper is published every Friday. Once described by the *Time* magazine as a "newspaper that wants to change Mozambique", *@Verdade* is a developmental channel meant to educate and raise the consciousness of Mozambicans concerning their rights. In an interview with Erik Charas, founder and director of *@Verdade*, during the fieldwork, he pointed out the paper's mission is "to intervene in the process of social development of Mozambique through the use of free information and technology". The paper's goal is to "feed the brain" of people who barely manage to "feed the stomach". Outlining the philosophy behind *@Verdade*, Erik Charas pointed out that "in a country where the normal retail price of any other newspaper is equivalent to the price of eight pieces of bread, or a month of mobile phone access, Mozambicans should not be forced to choose between having access to the news or buy bread". Running under the catchy Portuguese slogan, *"A Verdade Não Tem Preço"*, loosely translated to mean "The Truth is Priceless", its print run oscillates between 20,000 and 50,000, although the paper is read by about 400,000 people per week. It has the biggest readership base in Mozambique. *@Verdade* also produces an online edition, downloadable in PDF format. The newspaper also relies heavily on its Facebook page (Jornal@Verdade). By June 2013, *@Verdade* had 33,278 likes and 11,568 people were talking about the paper on Facebook. Although Facebook is predominantly English, it is noteworthy to highlight on the Jornal@Verdade page all the postings are written using Portuguese. The paper also has a Twitter account (verdadem) and a YouTube channel. All these channels are well linked with each other and fully integrated into the printed version. It is arguable that *@Verdade*'s creative appropriation of a myriad of technologies has been necessitated by the shaping impact of the socio-political and economic context. Mozambique has a long history of newspapers distributed via fax and email.

The newspaper generates its income through advertising and partnerships with international donors. Its print version carries 32 pages in full colour. It has several sections, of which the most popular is the Cidadão Repórter (Citizen Reporter) section where people can report on corruption and service delivery challenges via email or Short Message Services (SMS).[5] This highlights the paper's innovative use of crowd-sourcing techniques to gather news from the ground. Such an innovation allows the paper to play a "midwife" role between the state and citizens by following up on public complaints and thereby putting pressure on the relevant authorities. The influential newspaper has brought several cases of corruption and service delivery challenges to the attention of government authorities. Explaining the philosophy and rationale behind the introduction of interactive platforms during the face-to-face interview, Eric Charas said: "*@Verdade* was designed and set out to be a tool for development of the citizen, the human being who is entitled to be an active participant of their country's economy simply by being informed. By being able to take or make informed decisions. By being able to speak and be heard." This kind of public journalism has yielded fruits for the once disengaged and apathetic citizens in Mozambique. In one such scheme, *@Verdade* carried stories from electricity users whose home appliances were breaking down because of power surges; this forced an existing but barely known sector regulator to convene public meetings to address the problem. Although it is too early to highlight the shortcomings of *@Verdade*'s version of institutionalized citizen journalism, it is fair to argue that in a country where 70 per cent of mobile phone subscribers are based in the capital city its participatory journalism promotes "elite conversations". In short, it excludes the digitally disconnected and rural people from participating in the mediated public sphere.

The use of a multiple platform dissemination strategy has seen "citizen journalists" filing stories and commenting through SMS or through Facebook from places where the paper is not even distributed. SMS messages are popular because they are much cheaper than voice calls. Although the paper has managed to engage in multi-format storytelling, it is important to point out that news editors retain editorial control over the selection of postings on Whatsapp,[6] Blackberry Messenger (BBM)[7] and SMS which see the light of day in the print version and moderation of user-generated content on social media platforms. Another shortcoming of the experiment relates to the unaffordability and lack of access to smartphones and laptops for ordinary Mozambicans which bars them from participating in the mediated public spheres. The pervasive "digital divide" along geographical, class and gender lines means that those with access to the means of symbolic reproduction (i.e. new media technologies) are in a position to shape the news agenda unlike those who are disconnected from the news production loop. Further, given the fact that the internet is dominated by English language as a medium of engagement, very few people who are literate in English are able to engage on Facebook and Twitter in Mozambique. Arguably, it is too early to dismiss the experiment as digital boosterist rhetoric, although participation on social media platforms remains skewed in favour of the information-rich.

The Creative Appropriation of New Media Technologies in Everyday News-making Routines

Given its not-for-profit business model, *@Verdade*, unlike commercial newspapers, is able to experiment with different kinds of new media technologies without endangering its financial position. Over the years, the newspaper has experimented with Ushahidi, SMS, email news alerts and at the time of this investigation they were implementing the "Citizen Desk" project. Both professional and citizen journalists are using these tools to engage in participatory journalism. The use of mobile phones and SMS have proved popular in a country where internet penetration is still low compared to the proliferation of mobile technologies. Thus before rushing to generalize on the limited use of new media technologies in resource-constrained societies, we need to acknowledge pockets of "digital native" journalists sprouting across Africa. This chimes with Accone's (2000, 69) point that "African journalists should hardly be viewed as second class Netizens. They have moulded internet tools to suit their specific needs, devised ingenious technical solutions to overcome the idiosyncrasies of their situations". In the case of *@Verdade*, the creative appropriation of technologies has greatly enriched its news production and distribution processes. Whereas before the advent of interactive technologies journalists in Africa, in general, and Mozambique, in particular, had to travel long distances in search of stories, expending enormous amounts of financial, human and technical resources, nowadays story ideas are easily "crowd-sourced" on social media platforms before they are cleansed using tools such as Storify.

One journalist who regularly crowd-sources ideas and content before writing up his copy puts it as follows:

> I regularly post my initial story angles on our Facebook page inviting our readers to comment and give constructive feedback. I sometimes get breaking news from high-density suburbs from people whom I have never met in real life. I then use these story leads to follow up either through interviews or fieldwork visits to the affected areas. We also use Storify at times to clean and validate our stories.

Besides crowd-sourcing, the mobile phone has also become an indispensable part of journalists' day-to-day work. In an interview with a journalist, who was trained in the days before the World Wide Web, he points out the following:

> Traditional journalists in the field would write up the story on the computer, go to the business centre, print it out and dictate it over the phone. Now with a mobile phone, you can do all kinds of things like recording interviews, taking images and posting content on social media platforms.

This shows that technology is "socially constructed by actors through the different means they attach to it"—and has flexibility with regards to the capacity of users to interpret, appropriate and manipulate technology in various ways (Orlikowski 1992, 399).

Unlike traditional news-sourcing strategies, in the era of social media journalists highlighted that story ideas came from all kinds of people, thereby threatening to obliterate the oft-cited divide between "elite sources" and netizens. From in-depth interviews with professional journalists at *@Verdade*, it emerged that social media platforms are being incorporated into news production processes, for a myriad of reasons, including to uncover news tips; gather content for stories; pursue and build news sources; reach out and connect with news sources; friend and follow influential news-makers (politicians, businesspeople, celebrities, etc.); gauge the public mood about events on the ground; report and clarify rumours; create and circulate stories;

and explore significant comments and replies in order to get more updates and interact with a broad section of citizens. It is important to point out that social media platforms are complementing their traditional news-sourcing strategies in ways that were not possible only a couple of few years ago.

Overall, despite the problems African journalists face with regard to new media technologies, they are making every effort to use them for their professional functions. Given the vast nature of the country's terrain, which has seen newspapers distributed by road transport taking days or weeks before reaching their intended destination, *@Verdade*'s deployment of a multiple platform distribution strategy has ensured that "as news breaks out" those connected are able to follow them in real-time. This has broadened the range of options available for the reception of its content, thereby complexly narrowing and perpetuating the gap between the information-have and have-nots at the same time. Most of its readers are working-class people who live in high-density areas in Maputo. During the time of the research, the researcher witnessed public transport buses dropping off readers at the gate of *@Verdade* offices to fetch their copies before proceeding with their journeys into town. Further, young working-class people, especially those based in Maputo who are not on Facebook, can make use of the durawall dubbed the physical "Facebook wall", which is just outside the newspaper's head office. On the physical "Facebook wall", citizens are able to post news tips, post complaints on service delivery challenges and act as whistle blowers on corruption cases. This creative appropriation of an online Facebook wall and its recreation in the physical space, where "citizen journalists" can write or illustrate breaking news in graphic formats and other user-generated content, demonstrates as Miller (2011) submits, that Facebook is produced in particular contexts where individuals draw upon their own cultural resources as they develop genres of use in line with their needs and expectations. This demonstrates that technology is "constructed by actors working in a given social context" (Orlikowski 1992). The point here is that "the way forward is in recognising the creative ways in which [the news organizations such as *@Verdade*] merge their traditions with exogenous influences to create realities that are not reducible to either but enriched by both" (Nyamnjoh 2005, 4). Extending the argument on the determined spirit of Africans to participate in the digital revolution, Nyamnjoh (2005, 4) adds that

> because Africa is part of the world, and because its backwardness is less the result of choice than of circumstance, ordinary Africans are determined to be part of the technological revolutions of the modem world, even if this means accessing the information superhighway on foot, horseback, bicycles, bush taxis and second-hand cars, or relying on lifts and the generosity of the super-endowed in the latest sports and fancy cars.

Social media, in the case of *@Verdade*, plays an instrumental role both as a source and driver of news. A reporter at *@Verdade* captured it as follows:

> Social media has enabled us to engage in a "live" conversation with sources and readers who are now integral members of the news process. These technologies are also enabling news editors to track breaking events as they unfold from the ground. We are now able to break news online without waiting for the weekly news cycle on our Facebook and Twitter page. Sometimes ensuing debates on posted stories help shape our follow-up strategies.

Innovative offline distribution strategies (door to door, motor bike, and walk in and collect your copy) have helped the paper to get to an otherwise hard-to-reach audience, while its strong social media presence allows it to engage with online readers. With a largely offline readership, the mobile phone has played an important role in engaging readers and seeking reader feedback. Without taking the journalists' accounts of the effects of their own work at face value, it is crucial to note that the appropriations of new media technologies are not without negative professional implications. It has destabilized journalism's traditional normative practices through the invasion of personal privacy, plagiarism (Mabweazara 2013), the peddling of falsehoods, the inadvertent promotion of a "social media news culture" that ignores large parts of human existence outside of Facebook and Twitter, and the advancement of a "post first, verify later" journalistic genre (Mare 2013).

Decentring and Deconstructing the Newsroom?

The gatekeeping role of journalism is perhaps the most explicitly affected by technological developments, as digital technologies have begun to usurp some news-gathering and selection routines from the journalists' brief. *@Verdade* represents one of the first news organizations to promote an "open newsroom culture" where netizens who would not otherwise have entered a space of public deliberation are able to file stories. With the internet still predominantly a middle-class phenomenon in Mozambique, it is arguable that *@Verdade* promotes an "elite virtual public sphere". This study finds that collaborative practices between citizen and professional journalists have given rise to "'ambient journalism" (Hermida 2012) characterised by omnipresent, often fragmented, collective storytelling efforts. Bureaucratic newsrooms, based on formality, rules and regulations, office bearers and clearly defined chains of command which have tended to constrain journalists' autonomy and independence throughout the news production process, are waning. The converged newsroom has torn down the "invisible walls" that used to separate print, broadcast and Web journalism, bringing into existence highly complex multimedia products. Observations indicated that newsroom culture and routines have changed with emerging trends towards home working, offices in a flux and a culture of the "perpetual" present or what Mabweazara (2013, 146) refers to as the "tethering effect" of the new media. The flexible properties of the mobile phone and social network sites have made the boundaries between work and home become porous, leading to a situation of "perpetual present" at the office or simply "on-the-go newsroom". This is associated with users' desire for constant "on-the-go" updates—matching their greater mobility—and their wish to participate in the creation of content and to witness and share news. The heavy use of computers, the mobile phone and email technology have rendered "newsrooms" as we know them porous. As one reporter at *@Verdade* explained:

> For us, it no longer matters whether you spend the whole day in the field because the newsroom has since become more of a place to pick a pen and notebook. Otherwise with my phone and personal laptop, I am good to go. I can file stories and images from the thick of things. Long ago, you have to wait for the diary meeting to talk to the editor but now from conception until the time of printing, there is a culture of collaboration.

Another journalist, who is a cartoonist at the newspaper, also explained the changing working relationships and newsroom cultures as follows:

> The most recognizable change at the newsroom level has been the dismantling of hierarchies and gradual shift away from specialization towards "multi-skilled" journalists. Everyone from the Chief Executive Officer to the ordinary secretary in the office is able to file stories. News sourcing is now everyone's responsibility; it's unlike in the past when cartoonists were expected to sit on a desk and scratch their heads all day long trying to come up with lucid illustrations from story ideas.

It is clear from the foregoing that cross-platform content production is allowing journalists to move away from creating stories for a single medium towards gathering information in a content pool and disseminating it in a variety of formats. Newsrooms are increasingly turning "into an open, ongoing [collaborative] social experiment" (Singer et al. 2011, 1) that gives "produsers" (Bruns 2007) unprecedented access to the social production and reception of news. However, it is important to highlight that the digital divide remains real and affects ordinary people's participation in the digital agora in a variety of ways. Having access to new media technologies is not the only "passport" required to participate in the virtual public sphere, but other factors such as digital and English literacies, willingness to participate and affordability are crucial. The decentring of the newsroom, however, has come at a huge cost because the notion of the non-stop digital news cycle has created a kind of never-ending deadline that puts tremendous stress on reporters. It has also reconfigured newsroom relationships and traditions, creating fluid, learning by doing kinds of media organizations. It is arguable that newsroom creativity at *@Verdade* demonstrates that the organization's strategic use of new media technologies is currently shaped by internal dynamics and dynamics external to the organization (Manning 2001).

Conclusion

This study has shed some light on how journalists at a community newspaper in Mozambique are creatively appropriating new media technologies in line with their existing professional norms and practices, and how it is changing work routines and newsroom culture. It has shown that although *@Verdade* operates within a context characterized by a lack of a reading culture among ordinary citizens and limited internet penetration, its experimental new media projects at the newsroom level have resulted in unique, contingent and situated appropriations. The establishment of a physical Facebook wall outside *@Verdade* head office, which acts as an alternative public space for "ordinary citizens" to write story ideas or engage in whistle-blowing activities, highlight some of the context-specific innovations. The unique appropriation of user-generated content through newspaper sections such as Citizen Reporter, Citizen Desk and social media platforms demonstrate that there are pockets of African Net-izenship which are sprouting in different corners of the continent.

It has also shown how new media technologies have reconstructed newsroom routines while decentring news-gathering practices at the same time. The interactive and participatory cultures accompanying the appropriation of new media technologies are recasting relationships between journalists and readers. The paper has argued that the appropriation of technologies has spawned journalistic ethical transgressions especially related to the publication of unverified stories, plagiarism, the promotion of "elite conversations" and invasion of personal privacy. The main argument is that although participatory journalism has begun to blossom in Mozambique, so long as the digital divide (based on class, gender and spatial relations, etc.) continues to exist, the information-poor will have limited chances to participate meaningfully in the mediated public sphere. In a country with massive rates of illiteracy (not to mention digital illiteracies) and poverty, the interactive and participatory cultures discussed in this study may be "neo-developmentalist" clichés with limited applicability to the lives of ordinary Mozambicans.

FUNDING

This study was made possible by generous funding from the Open Society Initiative of Southern Africa (OSISA) and the Highway Africa Chair of Media and Information Society (Rhodes University), South Africa. While their support is gratefully acknowledged, the views reflected in this study are those of the author and not the two funding organisations.

NOTES

1. This is according to the www.internetworldstats.com as of 30 June 2012.
2. This was the theme of the Press Freedom Day Celebrations sponsored by Mondi Shanduka Newsprint Private Limited held at the Rhodes University, Grahamstown, South Africa, Albany Museum, 4 May 2009.
3. This refers to a wireless communications standard designed to provide 30–40 megabit/second data rates, with the 2011 update providing up to 1 Gbit/second for fixed stations.
4. Community can be defined in many ways, from time- and space-specific communities of culture and geography, to intentional communities or communities of affinity such as virtual communities or interpretive communities (Bender 1978). In this study, community newspaper refers to a non-profit-making newspaper whose audiences are concentrated on a particular geographical location, although its reach is not limited to that particular locality.
5. SMS refers to a text messaging service component of phone, Web or mobile communication systems, using standardized communications protocols that allow the exchange of short text messages between fixed line or mobile phone devices.
6. Whatsapp is a cross-platform instant messaging application for smartphones. Users are able to text messages, send each other images, video and audio media messages.
7. BBM is an internet-based instant messenger and video-telephony application included on BlackBerry devices that allows messaging between BlackBerry users.

REFERENCES

Accone, Tanya. 2000. "Digital Dividends for Journalism in Africa." *Nieman Reports* 54 (4): 67–69.

Atton, Chris, and Hayes Mabweazara. 2011. "New Media and Journalism Practice in Africa: An Agenda for Research." *Journalism: Theory, Practice & Criticism* 12 (6): 667–673.

Anderson, Chris. 2005. *An Analysis of Online Journalism, Professionalism and the Role of Expert Knowledge in the Collection of News*. 16 December. Accessed September 28 2011. http: www.indymedia.org/DeprofJourn.pdf.

Banda, Fackson, Okoth F. Mudhai, and Wisdom Tettey. 2009. "Introduction: New Media and Democracy in Africa—a Critical Interjection." In *African Media and the Digital Public Sphere*, edited by Okoth Fred Mudhai, Wisdom J. Tettey and Fackson Banda, 1–20. New York: Palgrave Macmillan.

Bender, Thomas. 1978. *Community and Social Change in America*. New Brunswick, NJ: Rutgers University Press.

Berger, Guy. 2011. Empowering the Youth as Citizen Journalists: A South African Experience. *Journalism: Theory, Practice & Criticism*. 12 (6): 708–726.

Berger, Guy. 2005. "Powering African Newsrooms: Theorising How Southern African Journalists Make Use of ICTs for Newsgathering." In *Doing Digital Journalism: How Southern African Newsgatherers Are Using ICTs*, edited by Guy Berger, 1–14. Grahamstown: High Way Africa.

Bruns, Axel. 2007. "Produsage: Towards a Broader Framework for User-Led Content Creation." Creativity and Cognition: Proceedings of the 6th ACM SIGCHI Conference on Creativity and Cognition, ACM, Washington, DC, 99.

du Gay, Paul, Stuart Hall, Linda Janes, Hugh Mackay, and Keith Negus. 1997. *Doing Cultural Studies: The Story of the Sony Walkman*. London: Sage in association with the Open University.

Fenton, Natalie ed. 2010. *New Media, Old News: Journalism and Democracy in the Digital Age*. Thousand Oaks, CA: Sage.

Giddens, Anthony. 1984. *The Constitution of Society: An Outline of the Theory of Structuration*: Cambridge: Polity Press.

Hermida, Alfred. 2011. "Fluid Spaces, Fluid Journalism: The Role of the 'Active Recipient' in Participatory Journalism." In *Participatory Journalism*, edited by Jane Singer, Alfred Hermida, David Domingo, Ari Heinonen, Steve Paulussen, Thorsten Quandt, Zvi Reich and Marina Vujnovic. 177–191. New York: Wiley-Blackwell.

Hermida, Alfred. 2012. "Tweets and Truth: Journalism as a Discipline of Collaborative Verification." *Journalism Practice* 6 (5–6): 659–668.

Jacobs, Sean, and Diana Duarte. 2010, 16 September. *Protests in Mozambique: The Power of SMS*. Accessed 20 March 2012. www.afronline.com.

Jordan, Marenet. 2013. "Poke Me, I'm a Journalist: The Impact of Facebook and Twitter on Newsroom Routines and Cultures at Two South African Weeklies." *Ecquid Novi: African Journalism Studies* 34 (1): 21–35.

Lloyd, Robert. 2011. *Countries at the Crossroads 2011: Mozambique*. New York: Freedom House.

Mabweazara, Hayes M. 2010. "'New' Technologies and Journalism Practice in Africa: Towards a Critical Sociological Approach." In *The Citizen in Communication: Re-Visiting Traditional, New and Community Media Practices in South Africa*, edited by Nathalie Hyde-Clarke. 11–30. Cape Town: Juta & Co.

Mabweazara, Hayes M. 2011. "'Wiring' AfricanNewsrooms: The Internet and Mainstream Journalism Practice in Zimbabwe." In *Cultural Identity and New Communication Technologies*, edited by D. Ndirangu Wachanga, 144–162. Pennsylvania: IGI Global.

Mabweazara, Hayes M. 2013. "Normative Dilemmas and Issues for Zimbabwean Print Journalism in the 'Information Society' Era." *Digital Journalism* 1 (1): 135–151.

Manning, Paul. 2001. *News and News Sources*. A Critical Introduction. London: Sage.

Mare, Admire. 2013. "A Complicated but Symbiotic Affair: The Relationship between Mainstream Media and Social Media in the Coverage of Social Protests in Southern Africa." *Ecquid Novi: African Journalism Studies* 34 (1): 83–98.

McNair, Brian. 2009. "Journalism in the 21st Century - Evolution, Not Extinction." *Journalism: Theory, Practice & Criticism* 10 (3): 347–360

Miller, Daniel. 2011. *Tales from Facebook*. Cambridge: Polity Press.

Moyo, Dumisani. 2009. "Citizen Journalism and the Parallel Market of Information in Zimbabwe's 2008 Elections." *Journalism Studies* 10 (4): 551–567.

Newman, Nic. 2011. *Mainstream Media and the Distribution of News in the Age of Social Discovery*. London: Reuters Institute for the Study of Journalism Working Paper. http://reutersinstitute.politics.ox.ac.uk/fileadmin/documents/Publications/The_rise_of_social_media_and_its_impact_on_mainstream_journalism.pdf.

Nyamnjoh, Francis B. 2005. *Africa's Media: Democracy and the Politics of Belonging*. London: Zed Books.

Obijiofor, Levi. 2003. "New Technologies and Journalism Practice in Nigeria and Ghana." *Asian Pacific Media Educator* 14: 36–56.

Orlikowski, Wanda J. 1992. "The Duality of Technology: Rethinking the Concept of Technology in Organizations." *Organization Science* 3 (3): 398–427.

Paterson, Chris, and Simone Doctors. 2013. "Participatory Journalism in Mozambique." *Ecquid Novi: African Journalism Studies* 34 (1): 107–114.

Saleh, Nivien. 2010. *Third World Citizens and the Information Technology Revolution*. New York: Palgrave Macmillan.

Schudson, Michael. 2005. "Four Approaches to the Sociology of News." In *Media and Society*, edited by James Curran and Michael Gurevitch, 171–197. London: Arnold.

Singer, Jane, Alfred Hermida, David Domingo, Ari Heinonen, Steve Paulussen, Thorsten Quandt, Zvi Reich and Marina Vujnovic 2011. "Introduction: Sharing the Road." In *Participatory Journalism*, edited by Jane Singer, Alfred Hermida, David Domingo, Ari Heinonen, Steve Paulussen, Thorsten Quandt, Zvi Reich and Marina Vujnovic 1–9. New York: Wiley-Blackwell.

Wasserman, Herman. 2005. "A 'Danger to Journalism'." *Rhodes Journalism Review* 25: 34–35.

Wasserman, Herman ed. 2010. *Popular Media, Democracy and Development in Africa*. London: Routledge.

Wasserman, Herman. 2011. "Mobile Phones, Popular Media, and Everyday African Democracy: Transmissions and Transgressions." *Popular Communication* 9 (2): 146–158.

SOCIAL MEDIA AND COMMUNITY RADIO JOURNALISM IN SOUTH AFRICA

Tanja Bosch

Using a qualitative approach, this article explores South African community radio stations' uses of the internet, particularly the online social networking sites, Facebook and Twitter. Specifically, it explores the extent to which these sites are used in news production, and whether there is an increase in organization on the basis of network sociality instead of identity politics or communal social relations. Focusing on three community radio stations in Johannesburg, Cape Town and Durban (South Africa's three largest cities), the article draws on anthropological methods of participant observation and qualitative interviews. The study argues that while the potential exists, in this case access to and the use of social media does not necessarily facilitate the formation of counterpublics or result in collective political action and networked activism. However, the technologies have impacted on the daily routines of community radio journalists who increasingly rely on the internet as a source of news; and in turn, their use of social media has led to greater access and participation for those audiences which are already online.

Introduction

Internationally, community radio practice has always been considered participatory, primarily because stations are usually owned and operated by community members, and on-air presenters. DJs and news journalists are ordinary citizens who are not necessarily professionally trained journalists. Similarly, social media is also considered a form of participatory media, and so community journalism, particularly when it converges with social media, might be seen as a heightened form of citizen journalism. Citizen journalism is defined by Atton (2003) as "a philosophy of journalism and a set of practices that are embedded within the everyday lives of citizens, and media content that is both driven and produced by those people … (and whose) practices emphasize first person, eyewitness accounts by participants" (267). Even though community radio news journalists are not professionally trained, they usually form a small group of staff at the station that exclusively produce and broadcast news. As such, they are referred to as journalists for the purposes of this article, as this is usually a full-time job even if in a voluntary capacity. In addition, the newsroom staff members interviewed in this study also self-identified as journalists.

This article explores South African community radio stations' use of the internet, particularly online social networking sites (SNSes) Facebook and Twitter. Through a qualitative exploration of three urban stations, each located in one of the three largest cities in South Africa, Johannesburg, Cape Town and Durban, the article uses participant observation and in-depth interviews to explore how community radio journalists use the internet and SNSes, and how this impacts on their daily news routines. In particular, the article asks whether stations begin to organize less along the lines of identity politics and communal social relations, and more on the basis of network sociality when they use the internet and, more specifically, social media. It also explores whether the internet could potentially facilitate the formation of counterpublics (Fraser 1990) and result in forms of collective political action or networked activism.

Community media emerged in South Africa within the context of the 'people's media' of the 1980s, which popularized anti-apartheid discourse. During the 1980s, community media included community newspapers, audio, video and student media, with strong leanings toward advocacy journalism because of their emergence within the context of political struggle against apartheid (Duncan and Seleoane 1998). Community radio projects arose as a result of the political and cultural struggles against apartheid of the 1980s, in which radio was seen to have the potential to inform and mobilize communities. After the first national democratic elections in South Africa in June 1994, the subsequent liberalization of the airwaves and the formation of an Independent Broadcast Authority (IBA), provision was made for community radio as a formal structure, intended to give previously marginalized groups access to the airwaves. There are three distinct categories of community radio stations in South Africa: "community of interest" stations are primarily religious, usually Muslim or Christian radio stations, but could also include stations that broadcast to specific interest groups, e.g. Fine Music Radio in Cape Town which broadcasts primarily classical music; "geographic community stations" are licensed to broadcast to regional communities which live within particular geographic footprints; and "campus radio stations" which are based on the campuses of tertiary institutions, universities and colleges, and broadcast primarily to students and the immediate surrounding geographic community. There are several key challenges to the continued success of community radio more than a decade after its creation. These include the production of quality content, issues of governance and community participation, achieving financial and social sustainability, and the ability to maintain independence from advertisers and government (Bosch 2010).

Information and communication technologies (ICTs) have been identified as having the ability to significantly improve the effectiveness of community radio stations (Girard 2003), and potentially help stations to address these challenges. The development of ICTs has been seen as potentially liberating for marginal groups that are not served by mainstream commercial media or who have limited access to these media. This includes the audiences of community radio stations, and there is a growing international focus on radio's use of ICTs, particularly community radio (see e.g. Girard 2001). ICTs are often seen potentially to create communicative spaces where community movements or social interest groups can share information more freely than by using traditional media (Kidd 2003). Kothmale Community Radio in South Asia is one successful example of a community radio station that has moved toward convergence and uses the internet to reach and educate audiences (Pringle and David 2002). In Africa the integration of ICTs at community radio stations is transforming the way these stations interact with their audiences, and redefining notions of community (Nassanga, Manyozo, and Lopes 2013).

There is the potential for mobile phones especially, to enable more substantial dialogue between community radio stations and their listeners, who often have limited access to fixed-line telephony. There is little access to fixed broadband internet in Africa with 0.3 per 100 inhabitants, compared to 27.0 in Europe and 17.1 in the Americas (ITU 2013). The widespread availability of mobile phone subscriptions increasing from 12.4 to 53 per 100 inhabitants in less than half a decade demonstrates the opportunity for mobile broadband access (ITU 2013). Mobile subscriptions in Africa are at around 80 percent in 2013, with 23.5 million subscriptions in South Africa (ABI Research 2013). In South Africa, most people either own or have access to a mobile phone (Finweek 2013). Internet penetration in South Africa is approaching 20 percent, with the internet user base having grown from 6.8 million in 2010 to 8.5 million at the end of 2011, but despite this growth nearly 8 million South Africans access the internet on their mobile phones (World Wide Worx 2012). While the internet and mobiles are two separate areas that cannot be conflated, the increasing possibility for people to access the internet using their mobile phones means that, for this study, both are considered. Mobile phones are considered primarily for their ability to access the "Web", particularly since respondents in this study frequently conflated the two, almost always referring to their mobiles as the primary tool through which they accessed the internet, in general, and their social media accounts, in particular.

The internet, mobile phones and other "new" media have the potential to create new opportunities for participatory democracy and to contribute to the growth of countercultures (Lister et al. 2003) or specific interest groups. These technologies, as part of a broader network of ICTs, may assist subaltern counterpublics to gain a foothold in the media and information landscape. The interactivity made possible by new media technologies has suggested metaphorical analogies with the democratic process itself, or Habermas's concept of the idealized public sphere (Wasserman 2005). Audiences are not passive receivers of media texts, but can actively interact with media texts and create meaning communally within social contexts and even take collective action against meanings produced by media (Croteau and Hoynes 2000).

In general, the use of new media has led to new storytelling techniques that engage the audience in more navigable ways (Pavlik 2001). For example, in South Africa several commercial radio stations provide multimedia versions of posted stories. Readers can subscribe to RSS feeds and receive updates, read the text versions of stories previously broadcast on the radio, or link to multimedia packages of stories that include digital stories or video television-style segments. Online forms of communicative engagement have facilitated ideas of collaborative and collective communication in traditional media organizations; with social media in particular demonstrating the ability and potential for those individuals who are politically engaged to simultaneously bypass and influence traditional information. This convergence of radio and the internet is interesting in that it offers stations opportunities to close the gaps between producer and consumer in the networked public sphere (Benkler 2006); as well as providing an additional medium through which to reach current (and potential) audiences. Increased access to online communication networks could be strategic in the formation of civic agency, extending the boundaries of the cultural public sphere so that community radio becomes a cultural space bringing together geographically fragmented but symbolically connected cultural netizens (Moyo 2012).

More specifically, social networking sites like Facebook, and the micro-blogging service Twitter, are increasingly intersecting with traditional mainstream news outputs. Social media have scooped traditional media in breaking news; and mainstream journalists often use these social networks to release news stories or to add detail outside of the usual news cycle (Bosch 2010). This means that news production is sometimes more participatory, with both journalists or news producers and consumers using social media to distribute news items. Similarly, the increased prevalence of the mobile phone has changed the practice of newsgathering in a number of ways. The most notable has been the rise of citizen journalism, and the spread of news without being subject to gate-keeping or editorial processes (Tacchi, Watkins, and Keerthirathne 2009). In Africa, in particular, the penetration of mobile phones above fixed lines has reduced issues related to the digital divide, as more people also have access to the internet via their phones (Donner, Gitau, and Marsden 2011.

This study adopted a qualitative approach, drawing on a purposive sample of three community radio stations in three of South Africa's largest urban centres: Cape Town, Johannesburg and Durban. The Cape Town-based station was a community religious-interest station, while the others were geographic community radio stations. Qualitative in-depth interviews were conducted with newsroom staff and volunteers, as well as with the station managers and programme managers of each of the stations. Interviews were conducted with 10 staff members from all three stations, on the radio station premises during working hours. In addition, newsroom participant observations were conducted with the stations in Cape Town and Durban, with the researcher "volunteering" to assist with news production over a period of one week. Observations continued in other areas of the station during the visits, such as the on-air studio and the kitchen during free time. Together with this, the researcher "followed" the radio stations and staff members on Facebook and Twitter in order to gauge their levels of participation on these social networking sites. This was an attempt at triangulation, to reduce over-reliance on interview data, though further research might conduct more extensive content and discourse analysis of the SNSes. Permission was given to conduct the study on condition of anonymity, as two radio stations were not willing to be named in the final report. While these stations may not necessarily be reflective of the practices at all community radio stations in South Africa, the selection of three cases presents us with a snapshot of the current situation with regard to urban stations' use of the internet and social media. In addition, the situation at community stations is not homogenous and tends to vary widely depending on various factors, which might include location (urban or rural, nature of city, etc.), access to funding, availability of and skill levels of volunteer staff, etc. However, the three stations selected are all well established with secure audience bases, and thus fairly "typical" of the range of stations one might find.

Discussion: Internet Use in the Community Radio Newsroom

There was internet access at all three radio stations, usually via a desktop computer, though the speed of the internet access, and the nature of connectivity, was variable. While some stations are connected via high-speed ADSL.

[1]lines, one was still using a much slower dial-up connection, on an older desktop computer. When asked about their use of the internet, respondents mentioned blogs

and websites first, before SNSes. One community radio station posts news items on a blog, which users can subscribe to via RSS, and also "tweets" their top news items via Twitter. The blog news items usually consist of the text of the broadcast newscasts, essentially a duplication of content.

The internet was listed as a critical tool in the community radio stations' newsrooms, as it was used both for newsgathering and distribution. As one journalist said, "I wouldn't be able to do my job without the internet" (interview, January 2013), while another echoed that "The first thing I do when I come to work in the morning is to check the internet to see what's on the news agenda for the day" (interview, January 2013). During my time in the newsroom, the computers were almost always displaying a webpage of an online news site when not in use, and when journalists were working on the machines they usually had several windows open, including Microsoft Word and an internet browser. Journalists said that they use the internet widely in the newsroom, primarily as a source of news, but also to corroborate news items or to add detail to news items heard on other radio stations. Community radio journalists said that the internet was a useful tool for identifying sources and interviewees, doing background research on these sources, and for generating story ideas. All the journalists surveyed indicated that their ability to work in the newsroom would be severely compromised by lack of access to the internet. In particular, they said that they would feel cut off and disconnected from international and national news events. While journalists mentioned that they relied heavily on the internet for research, they often displayed little understanding of how to evaluate sources for quality or accuracy. During the newsroom observations I noticed that they often relied on blogs and opinion instead of refereed sources, and they often generated limited data sources because of poor use of search techniques and ineffective keywords.

Mabweazara (2011a) has previously observed the ethical and professional challenges that have emerged with the use of the internet in the newsroom, especially the tendency to cut and paste material often without attribution, verification or attempts to talk directly to sources. Interestingly, in community radio newsrooms, this tendency to "cut and paste" seems to have been widespread before the rise of the internet, with journalists listing mainstream daily newspapers as one of their major sources of news. Alongside access to the internet, they list online newspapers as a major news source, and while they may rewrite and verify stories instead of simply "cutting and pasting", mainstream news sources still remain a major agenda-setting tool. The internet is widely used by journalists who were familiar with it before entering the newsroom, as a source of news and as a research tool. Desktop computers or laptops connected to the internet are seen as an essential professional tool, with a few journalists at one station even accessing the internet via their personal 3G-enabled tablets (the Samsung Galaxy Tab being by far the most popular tablet encountered during the study). Journalists' choice of internet-enabled tablet was usually related to their opportunity to purchase a monthly payment plan via various special offers, as they listed the prohibitive cost of paying cash for these devices. Radio stations did not assist in the acquisition of these devices.

As a result, it could be argued that community journalists are attempting to engage with new technology, but not yet managing to do so in meaningful ways. This raises an additional dimension of the "digital divide"—while the term usually refers to access to technology, in this instance we see that the notion of a "digital divide" can be broadened to include gaps in digital literacies. While stations are connected to the internet there is little or no user interactivity and nearly all of the news items are repetitious of mainstream print news items, with no evidence of any civic journalism or direct engagement with community members. In fact, in all the three cases studied, it seems as though access to the internet reduced already limited interaction with community members as potential news sources. Berger and Mgwili-Sibanda (2006) have demonstrated how small-scale print media across the continent have failed to use ICTs effectively and have not realized their potential to contribute African news content to global cyberspace. Similarly, South African community radio stations are not using the internet to share news with other community stations in the country; and they are not attempting to influence national news agendas by using their internet presence to elevate the status of local news stories. In considering the provision of local news via online platforms, we should, however, keep in mind that "the adequacy of news for local communities is also largely dependent on assumptions of homogeneity amongst local audiences who are increasingly fragmented into vertical interest groups rather than horizontal affiliations with local civil society" (Maher 2006, 8).

Community Radio Audiences and the Appropriation of Social Media

Before exploring how community radio journalists use SNSes, we should briefly consider community radio stations and their audiences, with particular reference to interaction via the internet or participatory forms of Web 2.0 such as social media. Table 1 shows the top 10 community radio stations in South Africa, rating them by number of listeners (RAMS 2012); and showing each station's social media profile as measured by number of Twitter followers, and number of Facebook members on the radio station's page. It should be noted that various programmes on radio stations often set up their own Facebook pages, which can be "liked" by fans. For example, Free State radio station Motheo FM has only 485 "likes" and no activity on its wall, but the much larger number of 1181 people have "liked" the page titled "Motheo FM Top 30

TABLE 1

Current status of community radio and social media*

	Radio station and province	Twitter followers	Facebook members	Number of listeners
1	Jozi FM, Gauteng	283	1767	406,000
2	Theta FM, Gauteng	No account	No account	345,000
3	Alfred Nzo CR, Eastern Cape	No account	302	337,000
4	Unitra CR, Eastern Cape	No account	20	326,000
5	Radio Tygerberg, Western Cape	1431	6529	291,000
6	Radio Khwezi, Kwazulu Natal	No account	30	288,000
7	Inkonjane 100.5FM, Eastern Cape	No account	No account	271,000
8	Motheo FM, Free State	404	489	256,000
9	Vukani FM, Eastern Cape	No account	No account	226,000
10	Radio Bushbuckridge, Mpumulanga	194	628	189,000

*AS OF 3 APRIL 2013.

chart with Shaun Dihoro", and the wall is active with listeners interacting with the DJ and each other, the DJ posting show content and advertising upcoming segments, and also posting photographs.

We should also acknowledge that the success or popularity of a radio station is not necessarily measured by number of listeners. The radio audience measurement system (RAMS) set up by the South African Audience Research Foundation (SAARF) was established to provide market research for commercial media outlets, and one might argue that it does not measure the community radio audience accurately, given the fairly small size of samples. The original focus was on the consumption of products and services by mass media audiences, and the data were to be used for target marketing and to help advertisers select media for advertising campaigns (www.saarf.co.za). It is useful to generalize about audiences at a national level, community radio audiences are often concentrated in particular (often rural or economically impoverished) areas, which makes the sample potentially less valid. As de Certeau (1984) writes, "statistical investigation grasps the material of these practices, but not their form; it determines the elements used, but not the "phrasing" produced by bricolage (the artisan-like inventiveness) and the discursiveness that combine these elements … the power of its calculation lies in its ability to divide, but it is precisely through this analytic fragmentation that it loses sight of what it claims to represent" (xvii). However, this article uses these measures as the only current and most convenient measure of "success".

What is very interesting here is that there is not a positive correlation between the number of listeners as forecast by SAARF, and the number of followers on SNSes. Fewer than half of the top 10 stations have Twitter accounts, and of those who use Twitter, many have very few followers on the social network. While Motheo FM in the Free State has 256,000 listeners, they have only 404 Twitter followers. Among the top 10 community radio stations nationally, there is an uneven use of social media, with some stations, like Theta FM and Inkonjane FM, not active at all on Facebook or Twitter, though we see listeners occasionally trying to reference these stations on Twitter by hashtagging the station. One example is a tweet which reads, "One listens to #thetaFm [*Theta FM*] and all you can say is, modimo bontsha sefahleho sa hao vaal. Vaal e hloka modimo man jerr, who rapes a 16 year old maar nxa", referencing an on-air broadcast and discussion of rape. This is translated as, "One listens to #thethafm [*Theta FM*] and all you can say is *God, show your face in Vaal. Vaal is in need of God, man. Damn, who rapes a 16 year old though? (nxa—clicking of tongue). This was in reference to a national conversation on rape taking place in print and radio after the violent rape and subsequent death of a young girl; and demonstrates how SNSes can become an extension of public sphere debate.

Similarly, Radio Khwezi has no Twitter account, but is referenced frequently, e.g. the user called MTN Radio Awards tweets, "Congratulations to Radio Khwezi, MTN Radio Awards Community Station of the Year finalist #mtnradio". On the other hand, stations with smaller audiences, according to SAARF, are fairly active on social networking sites, as indicated in Table 2. This is often linked to the socio-economic status of the region in which stations are located. Stations in affluent or urban areas might have audiences who are more connected to the internet via their mobiles or even have broadband access on desktop computers. However, even when stations are not members of SNSes, journalists who work at these stations and some of their audience members might be. When one of the country's oldest community radio stations

TABLE 2
Community radio stations active on SNSes

Radio station and province	Twitter followers	Facebook members	Number of listeners
1 Bush Radio, Western Cape	4067	1836	30,000
2 Radio Tygerberg, Western Cape	1431	6529	291,000
3 Jozi FM, Gauteng	283	1767	406,000

suffered financial difficulties and almost went off air, an outpouring of support on Facebook and Twitter generated enough international interest to elicit an interest from international funders (Mudzingwa 2012).

These figures, while high for community radio, are in stark contrast to figures from commercial radio stations. For example, national commercial music radio station 5FM has 243,205 Twitter followers, with Metro FM following closely with 71,686, Talk Radio 702 with 63,204 and Gauteng-based music station 94.7 Highveld Stereo with 58,646. Since many listeners tend to be cultural "omnivores" (Peterson 1992) and listen to both community and commercial stations, this trend is probably more reflective of listeners' engagement with stations rather than internet access.

When it comes to journalists' use of social media, Facebook and Twitter were listed as the most often used SNSes. Journalists had personal Twitter and Facebook accounts even in cases where their radio stations also had general accounts. They indicated that they checked these accounts several times a day, often leaving them open in windows minimized on their computer workstations, and returning to these sites often during the course of the work day. As one journalists said, "I'm always on Facebook. I check my Facebook every five minutes. I feel lost without it!" (interview, January 2013). When using Twitter, in particular, community journalists often engaged in forms of meta-journalism (Dvorak 2006, in Mare 2013), rating, commenting and re-tweeting or reposting in other spaces such as Facebook, the posts of other individuals and journalists from other media outlets. "Mass media news is based on a complex of newsroom routines and rituals, conditions of production, notions of professionalism and objectivity, rehearsed standards of writing and editing" (Atton 2010, 10). As a result, journalists seemed hesitant to list social media sites as one of their news sources, though online newspapers and websites of other media organizations were frequently listed as sources of news, as discussed earlier. Journalists mentioned that they often encountered news stories on social media sites, particularly Facebook and Twitter, but that they would then seek verification from more traditional, official and mainstream sources.

This does raise the potential agenda-building role of social media, as journalists indicated they would be more likely to cover stories that received extensive coverage on SNSes, saying that this indicated potential audience interest in those stories. "If people are talking about it on Twitter it must be newsworthy" (interview, January 2013). However, journalists raised the lack of professionalism and objectivity on SNSes as the main reason not to rely on them as primary sources of news. This highlights the potential for citizen engagement, but with challenges of the digital divide, this is problematic.

Despite their skepticism towards SNSes as news sources, newsroom conversation often revolved around what journalists had seen on Facebook or Twitter; and they seemed to use SNSes for story ideas. Sometimes this was by subscribing to tweets from other national and international media outlets or news agencies; but often, in the case of Twitter and Facebook, it was by picking up on posts by friends. Here we clearly see the role social media plays as a selective amplifier and filter of mainstream media content (Mare 2013), with community journalists often relying on this as a major source of news despite their assertions to the contrary. Journalists indicated that in the past, they would often wait for the daily newspapers to be delivered, to help with their story selections for news bulletins, but that now they turned directly to the internet, particularly SNSes, for a sense of the breaking news of the day. "I'm not sure why I bother reading the newspapers because by the time I do so, I'm already familiar with the stories from Facebook" (interview, January 2013). This filtering of news stories though acquaintances and people known to the journalists or those within their existing networks could limit diversity or reinforce prejudices (Sunstein 2009), or particular political perspectives. At the same time, this helps community radio fulfill one of its key mandates of engaging with audiences in participatory ways, and allowing audience members to determine content through collaborative journalism. With audiences able to contribute to setting the news agenda by tweeting stories to the radio station; or by the radio station picking up on tweets and other posts by community and audience members via SNSes. This use of social media also raises a dramatic change in the daily newsroom routine, with journalists now frequently checking their social media sites for news updates or breaking news; and spending a large proportion of their time in the office connected to and checking or updating SNSes on their mobile phones. During observations it was also noted that journalists often connected to SNSes during their breaks on their own mobile phones, and sometimes even interacted with their own newsroom colleagues via SNSes.

Journalists did not use SNSes as a tool to post breaking news as many commercial, mainstream journalists do, often live tweeting from events, press conferences, or live from the scene. Instead, when community journalists tweeted stories, it was often after these stories had already been broadcast, or to direct audiences to later news broadcasts. The function of Twitter in this instance was simply to repeat existing news broadcasts, instead of providing additional material not provided in news bulletins, and as such was almost always dated. While SNS could potentially be a vehicle for activism or communicative power—people's ability to act in concert, with action amounting to communicative action aimed at mutual understanding (Arendt 1970)—in this instance access to the internet is not revolutionary in any way for these community stations. While the internet and SNSes have, in some contexts, given rise to activism, particularly by social movements (see e.g. Wasserman 2005), for these community radio journalists, it is merely an informational tool and not a vehicle for networked activism.

In addition, journalists did not distinguish between themselves as individuals or citizens, versus their identities as journalists. They often blurred the lines by using one social media account, and using this to tweet in a private and a personal capacity. While they claimed not to rely too much on social media as a source of news, they often "tweeted" or "Facebooked" news content that they encountered on a daily basis, particularly when they held strong personal views on news content. Stories about rape and sexual violence, police brutality or government corruption were some examples listed by journalists, who used SNSes freely to comment on these stories. In these instances journalists saw SNSes as an extension of their broadcasts, and believed they were talking to more than just their friends and acquaintances, but also their radio audiences. They no longer see audiences in the traditional sense, where community radio audiences are organized around identity politics or communal social relations, but rather on the basis of networked sociality. Often their use of SNSes even superseded email, with most journalists using only the official station email account for work-related emails and to receive press releases, but their Facebook email for private and other emails.

The idea of participatory journalism, particularly through SNSes, is that it engages journalists and audiences, facilitating multi-directional communication between these two groups. However, traditional media organizations have developed models of audience-engagement that do not consider the audience as equal, and maintain the professional control of journalists in story selection and agenda setting. While user-generated content on SNSes could potentially bypass traditional gatekeepers and allow audiences to set news agendas, this content is still viewed by community journalists with some skepticism; and while they stay alert to trends on SNSes, it is not seen as a primary source of news, but instead a news source requiring further research and verification.

Community radio journalists have followed mainstream media's trends of using social media as a professional tool (Jordaan 2013), but it has not significantly changed their approaches to story selection or presentation of news items. SNSes represent the potential for the formation of counterpublics (Fraser 1990) or public sphericules (Gitlin 1998), though community stations, already often radical in nature by virtue of being alternative to mainstream, are not tapping into this; simply because the numbers of social media followers are not yet as large as the number of actual listeners. Access to SNSes has allowed community stations to look outward and situate themselves in a broader global context, but it has not necessarily changed the ways they report; though it has perhaps opened up access and participation for those community members who are online. "Anyone can write on our Facebook wall or Tweet us and sometimes we'll even read their messages on the air" (interview, January 2013). Gitlin (1998) has argued against the notion of a single public sphere, instead proposing the idea of public sphericules, comprising segments of the public sphere. The idea of counterpublics or public sphericules refers to the fact that there might not necessarily be one unified public sphere as proposed by Habermas (1989), but that regional media outlets could create parallel discursive arenas where matters of political and social concern are discussed and debated, with the formation of public opinion the end result. This highlights the purpose of community radio stations, with its confluence around identity politics and communal social relations, but we do not see the formation of these sphericules on social media, which has become merely an extension of existing broadcasts and existing forms of sociality.

Community Radio Journalists and Mobile Phones

In the discussion of social media, mobile phones emerge as a related topic, particularly as many journalists indicated that they frequently accessed the internet on their mobiles. "I'm always online, if I'm not on the internet in the newsroom I'm surfing the internet on my Blackberry" (interview, January 2013). Previous literature has shown that mobile phone technology may hold the key to bridging the digital divide, particularly the unequal access to the internet, in and within Africa (see e.g. Fuchs and Horak 2008; Aker and Mbiti 2010). In South Africa in 2008 when only 15 percent of households had a working computer, with 5 percent of these online, 62 percent of the population owned a mobile phone or active SIM card (Hyde-Clark and van Tonder 2011). In general, mobile technology may offer developing countries access to the internet in the absence of fixed lines or traditional internet access via computers. However, some authors (e.g. Chigona et al. 2009) have argued that mobile internet usage is low among socially excluded low-income groups because they do not have access to internet-enabled mobile phones. In the present study, journalists all had access to internet-enabled mobile phones, and in fact most of them owned Blackberry smartphones, highlighting the fact that community radio journalists might not always be representative of their target audiences.

A growing number of mobiles support data connections, and individuals accessing the internet via these mid-market handsets usually have no access to a traditional PC-based internet connection; although internet access on mobiles makes the assumption that users are familiar with computers, by using terms like "desktop" and asking for case-sensitive passwords (Donner, Gitau, and Marsden 2011). In the present study, journalists often listed their mobile phones as a valuable tool to access the internet, either because internet access was limited at their stations due to costs, or because the connection speed was too slow.

While this may raise issues for audiences' abilities to access radio station content via the internet or the mobile internet, community radio journalists identified the mobile phone as a key communication tool, an extension of self and a critical item for personal and professional communication. The mobile phone has "increasingly occupied a central position in discourse about participatory media in Africa, with the technology used in varying degrees, by citizens, to contribute to news-making and information exchange in influential ways" (Paterson 2013, 2). When funds allowed, mobiles were sometimes provided by the radio station as a loan to senior journalists, but were considered an essential tool, so in most cases the journalists preferred to pay for it themselves, and use their own personal mobile phone for personal and work-related tasks. In this sense, the technology begins to blur the lines between journalists' private lives and work identities, assuming a taken-for-granted role in their daily routines (Mabweazara 2011b). All the community radio stations in this study had landlines, but journalists raised the prohibitive rising costs of fixed-line telephony, which often limited the number of calls they could make or the duration of these calls. Instead of using landlines to contact sources, they often used the Short Message Service, popularly referred to as SMS or instant messaging services like Whatsapp or BlackBerry Messenger (BBM) to contact sources, at a much cheaper rate. While one might assume that it would be cheaper to make calls using fixed landlines, the mobile phone has the obvious advantage of the SMS and the culture of "beeping", exchanging messages via intentional missed calls (Donner 2007). The SMS is widely used by journalists to keep in touch with their sources and audience members. While not a social media, in the African context Paterson (2013) has argued that SMS is the dominant facilitator of new modes of participatory journalism, as it is perhaps more social than internet-based technologies which have little impact in a context where internet access is inconsistent. While SMS was often used to communicate with sources that did not have smartphones, journalists used instant messaging services to communicate with each other, and with their friends and families.

Conclusion

The digital divide is still a key issue for Africa, particularly in the exploration of the use of internet-based technologies for journalism. Internet penetration in Africa is only 15.6 percent, and 17.4 percent in South Africa—ranked 14th out of 58 countries (internetworldstats.com). However, the increase in availability and affordability of mobile phones has begun to change the way we have traditionally viewed the digital divide. Africa has 650 million mobile phone subscribers, more than either the United States or the European Union (Falk 2012), and people are increasingly using their phones to access the internet. In South Africa, low download speeds and high costs have led to fewer people using fixed-line internet connections, instead preferring to connect through mobile devices (Sapa 2012). This rise of mobile internet usage has been listed as one possible solution to the challenge of the digital divide, but still raises issues of access to internet-enabled handsets and the costs of data. Despite variable access, community radio stations in South Africa use social media widely to connect with their audiences, as an extension of the airwaves, and community radio stations have begun to model this trend. They no longer see audiences in the traditional sense, where community radio audiences are organized around identity politics or communal social relations, but rather on the basis of networked sociality. The audience is not necessarily the target audience as defined by the radio station, but could comprise individuals that interact with the station or journalists primarily via SNSes beyond the traditional target community, redefining the traditional notions of "community".

While this does not necessarily imply greater participatory engagement with audiences, commercial radio stations use SNSes widely as an extension of their broadcasting, to engage radio audiences and to extend broadcasts and conversation beyond the airwaves. Community radio stations have begun to do this, but probably because their audiences are constituted from lower socio-economic groups with less access to traditional internet or mobile-enabled phones, they have had a lower success rate. Community radio journalists have followed mainstream media's trends of using social media as a professional tool but it has not significantly changed their approaches to story selection or presentation of news items. However, community radio journalists identify the internet in general, and SNSes in particular, as key professional tools. Both are used widely by these community radio journalists as they begin to organize more along the basis of network sociality than identity politics or community social relations; and their use of SNSes has impacted their daily news routines.

FUNDING

The research was made possible by funding from the National Research Foundation.

NOTE

1. Asymmetric digital subscriber line (ADSL) is a type of digital subscriber line that enables faster data transmission over telephone lines than a modem can provide.

REFERENCES

ABI Research. 2013. *Cellular Penetration in Africa Expected to Surpass 80%*. http://www.abiresearch.com/press/cellular-penetration-in-africa-expected-to-surpass.

Aker, Jenny, and Isaac. Mbiti. 2010. *Mobile Phones and Economic Development in Africa*. Centre for Global Development Working Paper no. 211. http://papers.ssrn.com/sol3/papers.cfm?abstract_id=1693963.

Arendt, Hannah. 1970. "In Friedland, Lewis et al. "The Networked Public Sphere." *Javnost* 13 (4): 5–26.

Atton, Chris. 2003. "What is Alternative Journalism?" *Journalism* 4 (3): 267–272.

Atton, Chris. 2010. "News Cultures and New Social Movements: Radical Journalism and the Mainstream Media." *Journalism Studies* 3 (4): 491–505.

Benkler, Yochai. 2006. *The Wealth of Networks*. New Haven: Yale University Press.

Berger, Guy, and Fortune. Mgwili-Sibanda eds. 2006. *What the Newsroom knows: Managing knowledge within African newspapers*. Grahamstown, South Africa: Highway Africa.

Bosch, Tanja. 2010. "Community Radio in South Africa 15 Years After Democracy." In *The Citizen in Communication*, edited by Nathalie. Hyde-Clarke. Johannesburg: Unisa Press.

Chigona, Wallace, Darry Beaukes, Junaid Vally, and Maureen Tanner. 2009. "Can Mobile Internet Help Alleviate Social Exclusion in Developing Countries?" *EJISDC* 36 (7): 1–16.

Croteau, David, and William. Hoynes. 2000. *Media/Society*. Thousand Oaks, CA: Pine Forge Press.

de Certeau, Michel. 1984. *The Practice of Everyday Life*. Berkeley, CA: University of California Press.

Donner, Jonathan. 2007. "The Rules of Beeping: Exchanging Messages via Intentional 'Missed Calls' on Mobile Phones." *Journal of Computer-Mediated Communication* 13 (1): 1–22.

Donner, Jonathan, Shikoh. Gitau, and Gary. Marsden. 2011. "Exploring Mobile-only internet use: Results of a Training Study in Urban South Africa." *International Journal of Communication* 5: 574–597.

Duncan, Jane, and Mandla. Seleoane. 1998. *Media and democracy in South Africa*. Johannesburg: Human Sciences Research Council.

Tyler, Falk. 2012. African Has More Mobile Phone Users than the US or EU. http://www.smartplanet.com/blog/bulletin/africa-has-more-mobile-phone-users-than-the-us-or-eu/9053

Finweek. 2013. http://finweek.com/2013/01/22/mobile-phone-usage-in-sa/

Fraser, Nancy. 1990. "Rethinking the Public Sphere: A Contribution to the Critique of Actually Existing Democracy." *Social Text* 25 (25 (26)): 56–80.

Fuchs, Christian, and Eva Horak. 2008. "Africa and the Digital Divide." *Telematics and Informatics* 25 (2): 99–116.

Gitlin, Todd. 1998. "Public Sphere or Public Sphericules?" In *Media, Ritual, Identity*, edited by Tamar. Liebes and James. Curran, 168–175. London: Routledge.

Girard, Bruce. 2001. "The Challenges of ICTs and Rural Radio." Paper Prepared for the International Farm Radio Workshop/ Information and Communication Technologies

Serving Rural Radio: New Content/ New Partnerships, Food and Agriculture Organisation, Rome. http://www.comunica.org/tampa/challenge.htm.

Girard, Bruce. ed. 2003. *The One to Watch: Radio, New ICTs and Interactivity*. Rome: Food and Agriculture Organization of the United Nations.

Habermas, Jurgen. 1989. *The Structural Transformation of the Public Sphere*. Cambridge, MA: MIT Press.

Hyde-Clarke, Nathalie and Tamsin Van Tonder. 2011. "Revisiting the 'Leapfrog' Debate in Light of Current Trends of Mobile Phone Internet Usage in the Greater Johannesburg area, South Africa." *Journal of African Media Studies* 3 (2): 263–276.

ITU, International Telecommunication Union. 2013. http://www.itu.int/ITU-D/ict/statistics/at_glance/KeyTelecom.html.

Jordaan, Marenet. 2013. "Poke me, I'm a journalist: The impact of Facebook and Twitter on Newsroom Routines and Cultures at two South African Weeklies." *Ecquid Novi: African Journalism Studies* 34 (1): 21–35.

Kidd, Dorothy. 2003. "Indymedia.org—A New Communications Commons." In *Cyberactivism —Online Activism in Theory and Practice*, edited by Martha. McCaughey and Michael. Ayers, 47–69. New York & London: Routledge.

Lister, Martin, Jon. Dovey, Seth. Giddings, Iain. Grant, and Kieran. Kelly. 2003. *New Media: A Critical Introduction*. London & New York: Routledge.

Maher, Vincent. 2006. *Towards a Critical Media Studies Approach to the Blogosphere*. http://vincentmaher.com/papers/VMO-01.pdf.

Mabweazara, Hayes M. 2011a. "The Internet in the Print Newsroom: Trends, Practices and Emerging Cultures in Zimbabwe." In *Making Online News, Volume 2: Newsroom Ethnographies in the Second Decade of Internet Journalism*, edited by D. Domingo and C. Paterson, 57–69. New York: Peter Lang.

Mabweazara, Hayes M. 2011b. "Between the Newsroom and the Pub: the Mobile Phone in the Dynamics of Everyday Mainstream Journalism Practice in Zimbabwe." *Journalism: Theory, Practice & Criticism* 12 (6): 692–707.

Mare, Admire. 2013. "A Complicated but Symbiotic Affair: The Relationship Between Mainstream Media and Social Media in the Coverage of Social Protests in Southern Africa." *Ecquid Novi: African Journalism Studies* 34 (1): 83–98.

Moyo, Last. 2012. "Community Radio and Cultural Citizenship: Reflections on Radio Islam and Democratic Citizenship in South Africa." In *Community Radio in the Twenty-First Century*, edited by J. Gordon, 303–320. Oxford: Peter Lang.

Mudzingwa, Davison. 2012. *Social Media Shows Support for Africa's Oldest Community Station*. http://www.ipsnews.net/2012/02/social-media-shows-support-for-africarsquos-oldest-community-station/.

Nassanga, Goretti Linda, Manyozo, Linje and Lopes, Claudia. 2013. "ICTs and radio in Africa: How the Uptake of ICT has Influenced the Newsroom Culture among Community Radio Journalists." *Telematics and Informatics* 30 (3): 258–266.

Paterson, Chris. 2013. "Journalism and Social Media in the African Context." *Ecquid Novi: African Journalism Studies* 34 (1): 1–6.

Pavlik, John. 2001. *Journalism and New Media*. New York: Columbia University Press.

Peterson, Richard. 1992. "Understanding Audience Segmentation: From Elite and Mass to Omnivore and Univore." *Poetics* 21: 243–258.

Pringle, Ian, and M. J. R. David. 2002. *Rural Community ICT Applications: The Kothmale Model*. http://www.ejisdc.org/ojs2/index.php/ejisdc/article/view/43/43.

RAMS. 2012. *Radio Audience Measurement Survey*. Produced by the South African Advertising Research Foundation (SAARF). http://www.saarf.co.za.

Sapa. 2012. *South Africans Ditching Telkom, Adopting Mobile Internet*. http://www.timeslive.co.za/scitech/2012/11/29/south-africans-ditching-telkom-adopting-mobile-internet.

Sunstein, Cass. 2009. *On rumours: How Falsehoods Spread, Why We Believe Them, What can be Done*. New York: Farrar, Strauss and Giroux.

Tacchi, Jo A., Jerry Watkins and Kosala Keerthirathne 2009. *Participatory Content Creation: Voice, Communication and Development*. http://www.fao.org/docrep/003/x6721e/x6721e35.htm.

Wasserman, Herman. 2005. "Renaissance and Resistance: Using ICTs for social change in South Africa." *African Studies* 64 (2): 177–199.

World Wide Worx. 2012. http://www.worldwideworx.com/wp-content/uploads/2012/12/Exec-Summary-Internet-Access-in-SA-2012.pdf.

READERS COMMENTS ON ZIMBABWEAN NEWSPAPER WEBSITES

How audience voices are challenging and (re)defining traditional journalism

Hayes Mawindi Mabweazara

Using qualitative data drawn from in-depth interviews with journalists, this study investigates how leading print newsrooms in Zimbabwe are adapting to the wave of changes spawned by readers' comments on their websites. It specifically examines how newspaper journalists are handling the "new" context in which strangers contribute and respond directly to something they alone once controlled. The paper further explores the professional and ethical dilemmas emerging with the volumes of user-generated content posted on the websites and the approaches taken by newsrooms in managing and "gatekeeping" the content. The study generally observes that while newsrooms are still broadly adjusting to the influx of readers' voices in their territory, the comments are increasingly shaping and contributing to the dynamics of newsmaking in ways that point to an emerging ecological reconfiguration and recasting of dimensions of news production. In the same way, the comment forums embody spaces for public deliberation. However, the lack of clear gatekeeping strategies has opened floodgates of abuses and extremist views that pose serious threats to the core values of news as well as the normative ideals of traditional journalism.

Introduction

The Web 2.0 era has revolutionised readers participation and engagement with the news in hitherto unseen ways. The participatory cultures emerging with new technologies are offering "myriad opportunities for readers to participate and interact with the news". In particular, readers' online comments are proving to be a popular form of participatory journalism, giving readers "agency [and] authority to influence news making" (Hermida 2011a, 14). Audiences who until recently were imaginary figures in the minds of journalists, now clearly manifest themselves online in various forms, including commenting directly to stories, writing on blogs attached to news websites and generally challenging the journalist as the sole "all-knowing" purveyor of information. While in the past the participation of readers was circumscribed to letters-to-the editor in newspapers, readers' online comments have become nearly ubiquitous, providing one of the most pragmatic and influential attributes of the interactive functionality of the digital era. As Reich (2011, 113) tells us: "No other forum has been so open, offering such an immediate and unedited access to any citizen wishing to express a view about specific news as it unfolds".

However, the implications of user comments for traditional journalism have received limited scholarly attention. While a sizeable amount of research on participatory practices and cultures is emerging mainly from Western scholarship, empirical evidence on emerging practices in Africa and the wider global South is generally lacking. It remains particularly unclear how African mainstream journalism is adapting to the implications of this popular audience participatory platform despite the fact that newsrooms on the continent are embracing the "promise" of new technologies in various ways (see Mabweazara, Mudhai, and Whittaker 2014). Indeed, "[t]he impact of the Internet has been as significant on media consumption as it has on production" (Accone 2000, 69).

This research lacuna has often meant that developments in African journalism are all too often measured against the backdrop of Western advances (professional and otherwise), this tends to overlook local idiosyncrasies and contextual factors that shape and underlie journalistic cultures in Africa. These factors include the socio-political, economic and institutional contexts that are markedly different from those in the West—often less clear-cut and resistant to any attempts to simplify them (Atton and Mabweazara 2011).

This study, therefore, seeks to contribute an African, particularly Zimbabwean, perspective of how mainstream journalists are embracing readers' online comments. It draws its empirical evidence from leading print newsrooms selected from the dominant state-controlled Zimbabwe Newspapers Group (Zimpapers) and the small but powerful privately owned Alpha Media Holdings (AMH) to examine how journalists are adapting and adjusting to the participatory cultures and user-generated content (UGC) associated with online readers' comments. The study specifically explores how the newsrooms (and their journalists) are embracing readers' comments as part of their everyday news-making culture, as well as the resulting professional and ethical concerns. It also explores the newsrooms' approaches to managing and "gatekeeping" the comments.

The study is underpinned by the view that changes in (African) newsrooms, including the adoption of interactive and participatory practices, never occurs in a vacuum, rather multiple contextual factors come into play to shape and structure journalists' attitudes, adoption practices and appropriations. To underscore this conceptual point of departure, the study draws on a constructivist approach to technology, which understands the appropriation of user comments in newsrooms "as a socially constructed multifaceted reality, and not a monolithic element that … imposes its own logic to … media companies" (Domingo 2008, 19) as technological determinists would suggest. The study demonstrates that interactive digital technologies associated with online user comments are, in fact, socially and culturally shaped and that the nature and form of the appropriation of these spaces is inextricably embedded in the context in which they are situated.

Context of Study: The Adoption of Web User Comments in Zimbabwean Print Newsrooms

While all the newspapers in Zimbabwe assumed an online presence in the late 1990s and have always devoted space for letters-to-the-editor, they have generally been slow to "seize opportunities for audience interaction afforded by the Internet" (Singer 2009, 481). For several years the Zimbabwean mainstream press did not prioritise interactivity on their newspaper websites.[1] However, around 2007, following the lead from international trends, including the interactive practices that emerged with news websites established by exiled Zimbabwean journalists post-2000, AMH's newspapers took the lead in the adoption of readers' comments. It refurbished and furnished all its newspaper websites with interactive features that enable readers to comment and contribute content directly to the newspapers (Mabweazara 2014). Explaining the reasoning behind these developments, AMH's editor-in-chief rhapsodised: "We are upping our game to ensure that we don't disappoint our readers who are yearning for lively commentary and *groundbreaking open journalism in which readers are not mere audiences, but active participants in content sourcing and formulating debate*" (emphasis added).[2]

This transition marked a key stage in adoption of participatory journalism in Zimbabwe. The interactive features of newspaper websites represented a marked "cultural" shift from the tightly controlled participatory antecedents such as letters-to-the-editors, rooted in the traditional top-down approach to news production, especially in the state-controlled press. By "letting the public into the previously closed world of journalism" (Hermida 2011b, 178), an avalanche of comments and discussions from readers of all socio-political dispositions strewn across the globe flooded the news websites. Unlike the letters-to-the-editor, online comments made it possible to present, within the same edition, the reactions of readers who also respond to and question one another. Thus, in the words of Singer et al. (2011, 7), journalists who have long cultivated "a professional distance from their readers and sources [have found] themselves integrated into a network in which the distances have collapsed".

It is, however, important to examine the adoption of interactivity and readers' comments by AMH in the light of the socio-political context in which they were introduced—a period during which Zimbabwe went through political turmoil following disputed presidential elections. During this period journalists generally faced challenges in accessing information as a result of the polarised political environment governed by stringent media laws (Mabweazara 2011). In this crisis period, as Moyo (2009, 561) observes, "news websites, including those that belong to mainstream newspapers … sought to get leads and insights from their readers to help them cover this complex political impasse". Thus, the early adoption of interactivity and UGC by AMH was not merely a shift towards global journalistic trends, but also an innovative attempt to access information in a context where the free flow of information was tightly controlled.

After an initial phase of resistance and scepticism, in 2010 Zimpapers followed the developments at AMH, "beginning with an initial overhaul of its newspapers' websites to incorporate interactive features" (Mabweazara 2014, 67). Although Zimpapers' slow adoption of interactive digital platforms can fairly be attributed to the prolonged economic challenges faced by the country since the turn of the century, it was also directly connected to its "innate culture of conservatism" and general concerns about the public's responses to its partisan editorial content (Mabweazara 2011).[3]

However, the radical shift from a deep-rooted conservative "top-down" news culture (Mabweazara 2014) in which readers' voices have traditionally been addressed in a tokenistic fashion via the letters-to-the-editor sections of the newspapers, clearly demonstrates the fear of "court[ing] obscurity and potential irrelevance" (Peters 2011, 155) by disregarding the changes and dynamics ushered by developments in interactive digital technologies. As Zimpapers' group online editor explained: "The changes in the media industry the world over cannot be ignored ... times are changing. It's clear people want their input; opinions considered. The changes were inevitable ... *We just had to move with the times*" (emphasis added).

Although both Zimpapers and AMH had mixed motives in adopting interactivity, as part of concerted efforts to participate actively in the digital revolution, in 2011 they both hired group online editors "with a number of evolving responsibilities, including repurposing print content for the Web; using social media to engage and deliver content to their audiences; as well as filtering user-generated content emerging from [the newspapers' interactive platforms]" (Mabweazara 2013, 137). These online editors work closely with senior editorial staff, in ensuring that the digital platforms of each newspaper reflect the editorial thrust of the news organisation, as well as offer engaging interactivity that enrich user experience (Mabweazara 2013).

Overall, the structures in place across both Zimpapers and AMH indicate "elements of gradual transition and adaptation to the era of interactivity and participatory digital journalism" (Mabweazara 2014, 67). Although the news organisations are yet to standardise their online operational procedures, they are far from "passively awaiting external salvation" (Berger 2005, 1) and "should hardly be viewed as second class Net-izens" (Accone 2000, 69).

Understanding how readers' comments are challenging and (re)defining traditional journalism in Zimbabwe requires a brief contextualisation of emerging theoretical observations on user comments and participatory journalism.

Online Readers' Comments: A Brief Overview of Emerging Theoretical Observations

Although readers' comment forums on newspaper websites are still heavily under-researched, there is a general consensus among scholars that they have become one of the most pragmatic and influential attributes of the online era (Hermida 2011b; Reich 2011; Santana 2011; Singer et al. 2011; Canter 2013). As spontaneous, informal and predominantly anonymous public forums, they represent a "new opinion pipeline not seen in the letters-to-the-editors section of the printed newspaper" (Santana 2011, 77).

Researchers have focused on a number of areas that point to their growing significance. One line of enquiry has examined how comments are revolutionising traditional newsroom norms and practices by augmenting and reinventing the means by which they interact with their readers and sources, as well as the way readers interact and relate with one another (McElroy 2013). The interactivity and connections facilitated by user comments are seen as enabling journalists to access information, ideas and feedback from their readers in ways that differ markedly from the "arms-length" operations of traditional mass communication (Milioni, Konstantinos, and Venetia 2012; McElroy 2013). Scholars argue that the surge in user-led sharing and discussion of news stories allows "journalists to gather first-hand material" (Gulyas 2013), especially if they are physically remote from the scenes and issues raised by the readers. Gulyas further observes that participatory platforms can enhance the degree of authenticity in stories, as they take "journalists closer to [news sources] where the [stories are] actually happening" (272). In this sense, the comment forums are seen as "expand[ing] the range of participants available to engage in news [production]" (Bruns and Highfield 2012, 21).

Research into user comments is often connected to general discussions on interactive digital technologies and their influences on the practice and culture of online journalism. Pavlik (2000, 235–236) contends that the era of interactive and participatory cultures has seen the emergence of a "two-way symmetric model of communication [in which] the flow of communication is … much more a dialog between both or all parties to communication". For Pavlik, the interactivity of the new media is bringing about a shift in the relationships between or among news organisations and their publics. Writing from an African perspective, Mudhai (2004) similarly observes that interactivity is changing news production processes and our very understanding of who produces news. Moyo (2009) further suggests that the ability to engage with news and with other news consumers is giving African readers greater influence over the material covered in newspapers while at the same time providing journalists with an opportunity to access ideas and leads from the readers.

The participatory culture of interactive digital technologies is seen as giving users "the power to challenge professional media monopoly by setting the agenda and framing the news" (Milioni, Konstantinos, and Venetia 2012, 23). Bruns argues that through readers' comments, the initial news reports are "fleshed out, examined, critiqued, debunked, put into context, and linked with other news, events and background information". For Bruns, this process "externalizes and turns [news] into a widely distributed collaborative effort … which previously took place either entirely within the minds of active news consumers, or within small relatively isolated groups of consumers discussing the news of the day" (Bruns 2008, 178). It is in this context that Singer et al. (2011, 1) postulate that: "The twenty-first-century newspaper is essentially never complete, neither finished nor finite … Nor are journalists the only ones determining what gets recorded. A great many other people also contribute content, representing their own interests, ideas, observations and opinions".

This direct participation and engagement by readers is also tied to the deliberative potential of online user comments, which some scholars see as enabling citizens to challenge and collectively monitor traditional journalistic discourse by "acting as watchdogs of the watchdogs" (Milioni, Konstantinos, and Venetia 2012, 23). In the same manner, citizens are seen as directly confronting topics avoided by the mainstream media in contexts where editorial and political constraints weigh down on the practice of professional journalism (Frere 2014).

Researchers have also focused on the negative implications of online readers' comments for journalism. In particular, the underlying logic of "openness and participation" (Lewis 2012, 840) characteristic of the comment forums is seen as challenging traditional editorial "gatekeeping" structures and standards (Bruns 2008; Hermida 2011b). This has led to concerns about the anonymity, lack of civility and unruliness of comments, factors seen as major drawbacks of online comments (McElroy 2013). For Reich (2011, 104), "writing under pennames lowers both the 'intellectual level' of comments and user responsibility for them". They become "random rants which are neither policed nor engaged with by journalistic or editorial staff" (Bruns and Highfield 2012, 17).

These dilemmas are directly linked to the burden of moderating user comments. As Singer et al. (2011, 3) argue: "[w]hen journalism becomes 'participatory', the volume of transmitted information rapidly surges to flood levels, swamping traditional approaches to winnowing and the like". Bruns (2008, 176) further submits that in the interactive digital era, "gatekeeping" "as a means of ensuring broad and balanced coverage", is no longer strictly necessary as the "gates have multiplied beyond all control".

Beyond the foregoing concerns, some researchers observe that journalists' dependence on UGC in news reporting portends "the decline of the maker culture" as the ready availability of information generated online encourages journalists to become "data consumers rather than creators" (Peters 2011, 155). Locating this argument in the African context, where access to the internet is predominantly disproportionate, Mabweazara (2013) argues that journalists' reliance on readily accessible online information for story ideas tends to narrow their perspective. Individuals who actively contribute to comment threads "command the discursive field and set the agenda for issues" (143) covered by reporters, much to the annihilation of potential voices without the means or knowledge to effectively engage with or contribute to the discourses circulating on the forums.

Researchers have also questioned the one-sided nature of deliberations on comment forums. Canter (2013) notes that while the nature of participation on comment threads is an interactive one, it is mainly between readers "rather than being between readers and journalists" (615). She contends that while journalists "may be willing to let readers respond to, and interact with, already produced material …, they are less willing to give them any real influence over the news process by engaging or collaborating" (605). Milioni, Konstantinos, and Venetia (2012, 21) similarly submit that, "whereas users challenge journalistic viewpoints to some extent, this type of audience participation is not likely to render audiences co-producers of news content in significant ways". Thus, readers "remain essentially audiences for journalistic work" (Reich 2011, 102), hence the traditional mainstream media largely retain their control over content and participation on the forums (Canter 2013).

Methodological Overview

The research draws its empirical data from a triangulated qualitative multiple case (newsrooms) and multiple informant approach that deployed individual in-depth interviews with journalists selected from newsrooms across the dominant state-controlled Zimpapers: two dailies, *The Herald* and the *Chronicle*, and two weeklies, the *Sunday Mail* and the *Sunday News*, as well as newspapers from the privately owned AMH: two weeklies, *The Zimbabwe Independent* and *The Standard*, and a daily, *NewsDay*. The research was conducted between July 2012 and March 2013 in Harare, the capital, and Bulawayo, the second largest city.

In total 29 journalists were interviewed for the study. It is important to highlight that the selection of the participants was primarily underpinned by a concern to understand particulars rather than generalising to universals, in keeping with the assumptions of qualitative research. I was "concerned with *explanation* in a wider sense than measurement or causation" (Mason 2006, 16 emphasis original). However, following Wimmer and Dominick's (2000) advice that in one-on-one interviews respondents are selected based on a pre-determined set of screening requirements, interviewees were purposively selected using theoretical rather than random sampling. Of significance in the sampling procedure was the need to select journalists from key "beats" (politics, news, entertainment, business, crime/courts and sports) and newsroom positions (junior/senior reporters, desk editors, editors-in-chief and online editors).

Interview data provided in-depth descriptions and "insider" perspectives of practices and cultures associated with the adoption and appropriation of readers' comments in the newsrooms. The flexibility of interviews particularly enabled me to dig deeper into *why* and *how* individual journalists (and their respective newsrooms) negotiate their way around readers' online comments and the implications for established practices.

However, given that in individual interviews, "people do not always say what they think, or mean what they say" (Jensen 1982, 240), it was essential to have a certain amount of knowledge about users' comments on the newspapers' websites, in order to be able to conduct a meaningful and focused conversation with the informants. Accordingly, to prepare for the interviews (and as I shifted from one interview to another), I identified pertinent issues about readers' comments on the newspapers' websites that needed probing in order to ensure that interview interactions generated relevant data. This *rudimentary* content analysis was particularly central in verifying and corroborating instances where journalists made reference to specific stories and user comments in their responses.

Given the nature of some of the data generated from the study and the likelihood of it being recognisable to other people, I have deliberately avoided using the journalists' names, preferring instead to use their generic titles in order to protect them from possible identification. Further, in cases where journalists specifically requested anonymity, I have completely anonymised their responses, avoiding any mention of their title or news organisation.

The rest of the paper presents the study's findings. The first part focuses on readers' comments as alternative channels of feedback and story ideas; the second part examines the deliberative and participatory cultures on comment threads; the third section discusses the threats and normative challenges posed by user comments as well as newsroom gatekeeping approaches. The paper concludes with a reflective overview of the study's findings.

Readers' Comments as Alternative Channels of Feedback and Story Ideas

Despite a dim view taken by a few veteran reporters, who considered the comments a "vexing distraction" (Santana 2011, 76), there was a general consensus among the journalists involved in this study that readers' online comments are increasingly moving centre stage, shaping and contributing to the dynamics of newsmaking in the newsrooms.[4] Many journalists across both the state-controlled and private press found them useful, and generally noted that despite the challenges and pressures embedded in embracing readers' voices, they provided valuable perspectives and insights critical in editorial processes and decisions. As well as providing fodder for scoops and story ideas, the comments were seen as helping them to connect with readers, "even if this entail[ed] setting aside time to sift through tons of dross", as one news editor put it.

Online comments were thus seen as complementing the wider ecology of resources at the journalists' disposal in gathering insights and feedback from their readers. Journalists across the newsrooms and beats highlighted that they made it a regular "habit" or "ritual" to read comments to their stories. As one desk editor at the *Chronicle* explained: "It is always interesting to engage with readers' responses to one's stories ..., *in fact, it has become part of my ritual every morning,* with the hope that I will stumble on something useful" (emphasis added). For the journalists, this "ritualisation" of readers' comments was hinged on their potential to provide useful feedback, which enabled them to gauge the popular mood and sentiments in response to their news content and broader socio-political issues. One senior reporter at *NewsDay* explained thus: "the feedback helps me gather ideas about how people feel, which is crucial for my next article. It helps my understanding of the type and quality of news people are looking for".

Journalists further noted that in some cases comments corrected misnomers and factual inaccuracies or even altered their outlook on the newsworthiness of a story. A senior business reporter at *The Zimbabwe Independent* gave a lucid explanation:

> We don't always get things right ... some comments are useful because readers point to shortcomings in the way we cover stories, and this can be useful for improving the quality our product, disconcerting as it sounds. There are a lot of people out there who know far much more than we do as journalists ... Some readers will tell you: "you omitted something in your story about corruption in this company, it's even worse in this other company ... you can phone so and so, he will give you more detail" or someone might comment "you got it all wrong in this story, you wrote about 20 per cent of what didn't happen, the real story is like this".

While journalists retained the power to decide which ideas to pursue, readers' comments were seen as broadening and extending their purview by "nudging them towards new and different ways to tell stories" (Santana 2011, 77). Some journalists gave specific examples of stories generated from readers' comments:

> I remember a few weeks ago, someone commented on my story about the corruption at the NMB Bank, he wrote: "do you know that the Reserve Bank of Zimbabwe has fined them for not giving financial results". I wasn't aware of that, so I immediately made a follow up ... and generated an exclusive story. (business reporter at *The Zimbabwe Independent*)

The interview extracts above point to the direct impact of audience's voices on newsmaking practices in the newsrooms studied by turning news sourcing into a disintegrated and shared practice in which a previously passive readership has "greater agency [and] authority" (Hermida 2011a, 14).

The influence of readers' comments in newsmaking processes also spilled into editorial meetings. Participants in the study highlighted that senior editors increasingly evoked issues raised on comment threads in editorial conferences, often cautioning reporters or pointing to issues that require follow-ups. As one reporter at *The Standard* put it: "Time without number our editor-in-chief mentions readers' feedback in our editorial meetings, which riles most of us. Often there are warnings about the dangers of being used, poor sourcing or even embarrassing grammatical errors". This development further points to readers' voices inadvertently taking centre stage in the newsmaking processes by providing ideas that shape the news agenda of the newspapers as well as contribute directly to the generation of new stories. Although journalists remain in control of the news process, they can no longer claim exclusive access to "the truth", as news has become an open-ended "artifact", subject to challenge and ongoing critique by a public that offers multiple perspectives and responses from a variety of angles (Hermida 2011b; Milioni, Konstantinos, and Venetia 2012).

Although the integration of audience voices has not qualitatively tempered with the basic values and principles of journalism, which remain centralised under the control of professional journalists, the interactivity of news websites was generally seen as enabling journalists to harness "the collective intelligence and knowledge" of dedicated users who "filter the news flow" (Bruns 2008, 176–177) by highlighting and debating salient topics of importance to them. In the words of Bruns (2008, 178, emphasis added), user comments are turning news "from a relatively static product to be consumed by audiences into a dynamic, evolving, expanding resource that is *actively co-developed by the users*". We are therefore witnessing an ecological reconfiguration and recasting of dimensions of news production in ways that echo Sigal's 1970s' observation that "News organisations ... alter their procedures, and ... make innovative responses to ... novel situations" (Sigal 1973, 101).

Although questions of "access" to the internet and users' abilities to contribute meaningfully to online discourses have implications for the impact of news sourcing online in terms of whose voices dominate the platforms and are thus bound to impact on journalists' news agendas (Mabweazara 2013), the anonymity and dispersed nature of voices commenting on stories was seen as swaying journalists away from their recurrent sourcing of news (and comments) from the same elite sources. A senior business reporter at the *Sunday News* aptly summed up this point: "The people who always come to our mind are professionals or well-known figures, *but with online comments it's different, anyone with his facts right can throw in their opinion*" (emphasis added). Further explaining this point, a senior reporter at *NewsDay* stated:

> Engaging with readers' comments allows one to explore or think of several aspects of a story ... Angles to the story may be as many as the number of positions occupied by people with an interest in the issue at stake. *Readers' comments, when they are useful, help to reveal some of these angles, which can be initially overlooked.* (emphasis added)

These findings point to the emergence of a multipronged model of communication in which the flow of information is becoming a shared "dialog between ... all parties to communication" (Pavlik 2000, 235–236). This is particularly central in a context where information flows are generally restricted and censored such as in Zimbabwe (Moyo 2009; Mabweazara 2011). By appropriating readers' comments, journalists are, therefore, strategically locating themselves at *the source*, "where information is most likely to flow to them" (Sigal 1973, 11).

Deliberative Engagement and Participatory Cultures on Comment Threads

Beyond the direct professional implications discussed above, online user comments were also seen as embodying spaces of "unfettered" public deliberation, which, in the terms of the journalists, "complement", "extend", "enrich" as well as "tear apart" news discourses. Users' comments were described as generating hard-hitting alternative discourses that confronted issues deliberately avoided by news organisations in Zimbabwe. In the words of one senior journalist at the state-controlled *Herald*:

> Hardcore political discussion has shifted to the online forums ... Readers have taken it in their own hands to create their own narrative and provide the other side of the story. As you and I know, there is a limit to the issues that newspapers in Zimbabwe can write about.

Several journalists across the divide of the state-controlled and private press explicitly described the comment forums as having the potential to fulfil a deliberative role akin to the Habermasian notion of the public sphere, a normative ideal long lost in the morass of restrictive editorial policies and the general tight control and regulation of the media in the country (Mabweazara 2011). A senior editor at *NewsDay* aptly explained this point:

> These forums are abuzz with very critical commentary on the state's leadership, fiscal policy, land reform issues, and police brutality ... The critical issues that concern Zimbabweans, but which are not easily accommodated on our pages because of government censorship and harsh reactions to negative or critical publicity.

In the limited mainstream spaces for critical and rational deliberations, especially on political issues, comment forums were seen as a central place for citizens to exchange views on wide-ranging socio-political issues, especially when they offer a "substantial amount of factual information, and [demonstrate] a public process of weighing alternatives via the expression of issue positions and supporting rationales" (McElroy 2013, 756). As Accone (2000, 69) further tells us, the anonymous nature of "this new medium encourages debate. The kind of discourse that would never grace the [printed pages of newspapers], because users are comfortable expressing themselves freely under the guide of non-traceable nom de plumes".

While readers' comments are triggered by professionally generated news stories —often deeply polarised along political lines—they are seen as offering alternative discourses that challenge and usurp journalists' position as "agenda setters of public discourses subtext as well as watchdogs of society", as a reporter at the *Chronicle* put it. Journalists described the diversity of voices responding to their stories online as enriching public discourses by bridging the partisan and polarised editorial content pervasive in the country's media (often leading to its failure to address adequately issues of vital concern to the public). User comments thus offer an alternative "balancing act" to news discourses in Zimbabwe by allowing a heterogeneity of voices and points of view that oppose or interrogate the hierarchies of discourses in news stories. The potential implications of the intersection between journalists' news discourses and readers' voices for the formation of public opinion was highlighted by a senior reporter at the *Standard*:

> In a significant number of comments, readers tend to challenge our viewpoints or openly express their disagreement with the angles taken in a story, including the sources we use ... They also take each other to task and this has far-reaching implications for the reader as it culminates in "new hybrid texts" that collectively shape meanings on critical public issues.

This observation chimes with Bruns' remark that comment forums "offer a corrective, an alternative interpretation of [issues] by adding the backstory and providing further related (and often contradicting) information enabling readers to better assess for themselves and by themselves the quality and veracity of mainstream news stories" (Bruns 2008, 177). Thus, while the news media in Zimbabwe is heavily polarised and partisan, as already noted, the same news online is "open to a higher degree of contestation than is typical of traditional news media" (Fenton and Witschge 2011, 154).

However, that basic principles of practice remain in place was indicated by the one-sided nature of interactivity on the comment forums. Journalists highlighted that while user comments were useful on several fronts as discussed above, they hardly engaged directly with readers on the platforms. This points to the fact that Zimbabwean newsrooms (as elsewhere in Africa) are still broadly adjusting to the culture of interactivity, including figuring out how best they can actively engage with their readers in the true spirit of participatory and interactive journalism. As AMH's group online editor explained: "we are still exploring ways of engaging directly with readers without distorting the flow of the discourses on these forums … At the moment we are leaving everything to the readers, let them determine the nature of the interactions". This response relates to Frere's (2014, 250) observations that journalists "are uncertain as to whether they should enter into a new type of relationship with their public" in keeping with the cultures and practices emerging with technological changes in their newsrooms. Elsewhere Hermida (2011b, 181) also observes that "the notion of entering into a substantive exchange of ideas and views with users has not become part of the journalist's … mindset". The relationship "remains rooted in long-established power dynamics" (180) which reduce online comments to "listening devices [which fail to function] as devices for a dialogue between journalists and audiences" (181).

Some journalists, however, attributed the lack of direct interactions with readers to the widespread use of pseudonyms and the entering of false email addresses on the comment forums, which made it difficult to generate useful dialogue. This marked a clear distinction with journalists' use of other interactive platforms such as social media, especially Facebook, which provided scope for building direct intimate connections with readers and potential sources (see Mabweazara 2014). Consequently, the most direct form of journalists' engagement with readers' comments was in the moderation of the content. This echoes Singer's (2009, 481) observation at *The New York Times* in which she contends that comment forums were reactive places that did not include journalists beyond simply "monitoring for abuse" (I explore this in detail shortly.)

The lack of policy directions on whether journalists should engage directly with readers' comments for both the state-controlled and private newsrooms was also raised as a key impediment. However, some veteran journalists across the divide emphasised the importance of adhering to the key journalistic ethos of *detachment* and *impartiality* by not participating in the online deliberations. One reporter explained thus: "There is a risk of exposing your personal ideological position or emotions if you engage directly with these comments … As you know, we should always be seen to be impartial and balanced". This view further indicates a shift to the Web with a deeply ingrained "old media" mindset that "permanently" relegates readers to the position of "audiences for journalistic work" (Reich 2011, 102). Thus as Reich further notes, "comments leave the journalist in the traditional position of the lead singer, while audience members generally play the minor, faceless and reactive role of the chorus" (98).

Normative Threats and Porous "Gatekeeping" Approaches

Although online user comments offer a number of positive dimensions to the news culture in Zimbabwe, they are, however, not without negative implications or threats to established practices and cultures. As Canter (2013, 604) observes in the British context, the "rise in participatory journalism has led to new challenges for journalists as they [strive] to negotiate the often murky waters of user-generated content". In the present study, journalists pointed to a number of unsettling individual concerns as well as generic ethical and professional dilemmas emerging with hosting audience voices on their newspaper websites. While most of these concerns related to well-known challenges associated with the interactive and participatory cultures of the digital era, some were tied to local contextual factors, especially the consequences of opening up communicative spaces to an embittered public that has endured years of a closed media environment.

A number of concerns were raised by conservative senior journalists who described the permeation of audience voices into their routine practices as akin to ceding their journalistic "power" to a mass of unqualified ordinary citizens who "have, in fact, become de facto 'watchdogs' of [their] professional activities", as one veteran reporter at the *Chronicle* put it. Journalists generally felt uneasy with this new dynamic and pointed to its potential impact on their personal morale and credence as professionals. A key concern was around user comments' influences on the performance evaluation of journalists, especially those whose work was persistently subjected to the harsh scrutiny of the watchful readers' eye. As one senior reporter at the *Standard* explained: "One can never downplay the impact of consistent negative comments on the morale and ability of the writer. What's worse is that most of these comments don't go unnoticed by our editors". Similarly, an assistant business editor at *The Herald* remonstrated thus: "Some comments are … downright degrading and personal. In your mind you are thinking, *'if the editor-in-chief sees this then I'm in for a thorough hiding' … It can be quite distressing*" (emphasis added). Writing about similar experiences in the American context, Singer (2009, 482) contends that "the ethical transition from professional discourse to a far more personal one is proving difficult", as journalists and their newsrooms engage with an enormously diverse range of people online.

For a number of veteran journalists, especially on the state-controlled press, these deep-seated concerns pointed to an unnerving demise of their hegemony and monopoly over news. Particular concern was raised about how some comments negatively affected perceptions about the media by swaying opinions over given truths. By the same token, some comments were seen as challenging "the professional's" journalistic integrity in disconcerting ways. As one sports reporter explained:

> A lot of people now rely on our websites; they post comments and do all sorts of things with our news product. *If you lie or get your facts wrong, readers will take you to the cleaners. And editors are becoming very strict. If they see queries … or negative comments about your story, they will send the feedback to you and you have to account for it.* (emphasis added)

In this sense, readers are not only undermining journalists' "traditional position of influence and importance" (Bruns 2008, 173), but also propping up a heightened sense of professional vigilance and responsibility by directly criticising their work.

Beyond the above personal worries, journalists also alluded to a number of generic threats posed by readers' comments to established professional normative ideals. Some comments were described as careless expressions of frustration and anger with the country's politics and economy without any qualitative or rational engagement with the subject of the stories. AMH's group online editor stated thus: "We often say, just joking with colleagues in the newsroom, that Zimbabweans sometimes appear to be so wantonly angry ... There is so much anger online, and this manifests in unwarranted personal attacks". These concerns relate to Frere's observations about the "the bitter citizen" in Burkina Faso who uses online forums as outlets for various frustrations, targeting their anger and insults mostly towards the government (Frere 2014, 241).

While the incivility and unruliness of comments are common drawbacks of online user comments (see Reich 2011; Singer et al. 2011), journalists across the newsrooms also raised particular concerns about the hate speech and tribal slurs generated on comment threads. A senior reporter at *NewsDay* gave a detailed picture of these concerns:

> While it is important to be open-minded at all times, aberrant comments are such a distraction ... This is mostly the case in political stories where some readers drag in tribalism and it ends up a slinging match of "tribalists" one at the Shona end and the other at the Ndebele end.[5] In such situations, the issues that are central to the story get lost.
>
> Sadly, some comments are insults directed to the subject of the story or readers fighting among themselves. In the case of my publication, there are readers like Phunyukabemphethe[6] who is notorious for commenting on each and every story, always hurling insults and spreading hate speech instead of commenting on stories.

The widespread use of pseudonyms on the forums was particularly described as contributing to the dumbing down of the quality of user contributions online. As one reporter explained: "Readers find it easy to smuggle [*sic*] tribal issues on matters that are far divorced from it ... because they are under cover and difficult to identify". Thus, while anonymity has its advantages in contexts where the dangers of being identified are real, such as in Zimbabwe, it equally "lowers both the 'intellectual level' of comments and user responsibility for them" by creating a "disinhibition effect" that leads to "'a reduced sense of responsibility and less pressure to conform to societal norms" (Reich 2011, 104).

Readers' online comments therefore pose serious threats to the normative ideals and functions of traditional journalism in Zimbabwe. They "put pressure on long-standing journalistic norms" (Singer 2009, 482) and foster misgivings about their significance in the entire news ecology. Further, in a context where ethnic tensions are rife (and often marked by violence elsewhere on the continent), hosting divisive user comments on the news websites can inadvertently fuel and deepen tensions.

The normative concerns above were rooted in the moderation and "gatekeeping" dilemmas faced by the newsrooms in managing the UGC on their websites. The inconsistencies in the moderation approaches deployed across the state-controlled and private press pointed to challenges faced in applying traditional standards to the new "cacophonous world of participatory journalism" (Singer et al. 2011, 4). While there were clear differences in the attitudes and approaches taken by the news organisations, they both broadly preferred a non-moderation approach. This was particularly influenced by their association with the pervasive culture of censorship in the country, which they described as potentially damaging to their readers' loyalty. Embracing the open deliberative culture and UGC on their websites was therefore strategic, as AMH's group online editor explained: "we have deliberately, wrongly or rightly, let people talk because we don't want to be associated with the well-known culture of censorship … We want numbers to increase on our websites".

However, despite this non-moderation posture noted above, both news organisations claimed to be particularly vigilant with regard to incitements to hatred, abuse, crime or defamation on their websites. As Zimpapers' group online editor explained:

> We are forced to censor for foul language and information which is not factual because it is easier to be sued when a comment appears on the website …, we censor some words that we feel are abusive and not good for a family newspaper. But I have to admit … sometimes the volumes overwhelm us.

Online editors also claimed to keep a close eye on political content likely to trigger hostile responses from various centres of power. However, as already noted, there were divergences in the approaches taken by the two news organisations. While Zimpapers generally deployed an overt and firmer approach codified in a policy document for users posted on newspapers websites,[7] AMH took a more relaxed approach. These divergent approaches echo Deuze's (2003) view that news organisations tend to expand their operations to the internet based on their existing journalistic culture, including the way they relate to the public. Explaining the reasoning behind the setting up of a user-policy, Zimpapers' group online editor stated thus: "The policy is informed by our editorial thrust as well as the country's laws. People can sue us, so we ensure that as people comment on our stories, they know what is allowed and what isn't". The setting up of terms and conditions for users should thus be seen in the broader context of Zimpapers' work practices, "innate conservatism" (Mabweazara 2013) and deep-rooted reluctance to relinquish "power" to readers. Consequently, while there is a professed attempt to facilitate free expression on the comment forums, there remains a reluctance to surrender the traditional gatekeeping role (Hermida 2011b).

On the other hand, the relaxed moderation approach adopted by the privately owned AMH was obvious in the lack of a codified "gatekeeping" policy beyond an informal statement of appeal to readers to avoid posting "profane, tribalistic, racist, libelous or malicious comments" displayed on all its newspaper websites.[8] It is for this reason that most journalists at AMH were not clear whether there was any moderation taking place, as one senior reporter at *NewsDay* put it: "It's not clear whether we have a moderation policy or not as all the insults traded on the website float around unabated". However, despite this lack of clarity, it was evident that there was some degree of control over content posted on the newspapers' websites as noted above.

Across both Zimpapers and AMH, limited resources, including the shortages of manpower noted as militating against maintaining foolproof control over their comment forums. For example, at the time of conducting research for this study, Zimpapers' group online editor was singlehandedly responsible for managing content on the organisation's seven newspaper websites. Similarly, AMH's group online editor was responsible for overseeing content on the news organisation's four newspapers. This scenario reduced "gatekeeping" to a porous and tokenistic approach akin to what Bruns (2008) refers to as "gatewatching".

Conclusion

This study has examined how leading Zimbabwean newspapers and their journalists are adapting to the "participatory culture" associated with readers' comments on newspaper websites as well as the challenges and professional implications emerging with this new "media ecology". In general, the study demonstrates that although the newsrooms are still largely adjusting to the practice of interactivity and the permeation of readers' voices into their territory, the developments are influencing and challenging newsroom practices in ways that point to an ecological reconfiguration of the established news culture. Readers' comments are providing a useful extra layer of functionality that complements existing practices through providing story ideas, engendering public debate as well as "holding journalists to account" by exposing poor journalistic practice. In the same way, the lack of effective gatekeeping strategies has opened floodgates to abusive and extremist comments that pose serious threats and challenges to the core values and normative ideals of traditional journalism. However, while the study's findings broadly point to common approaches to online user comments across the state-controlled and the private press, there are variances in the moderation of UGC. Whereas Zimpapers generally deploys an overt and firmer approach codified in policy, the latter takes a *laissez-faire* slant. These divergent approaches affirm the news organisations' expansion to the Web based on their prevailing journalistic culture, including the way they relate to the public.

For both newsrooms, however, it is clear that the incivility and unruliness of comments are a key challenge. The newsrooms need to act swiftly to address concerns about hate speech and tribal slurs generated on comment threads. In particular, there is need to consider developing effective user-regulation policies that strive towards nurturing accountability among users without necessarily watering down or impeding discourses and deliberations. As Santana (2011, 78) advises, one way of "raising the level of discourse" demands tapping into the "wisdom of the crowd to decide which commenters should be heard and which should be muted". This also entails improving reader–journalist interactions in order to foster a robust participatory and interactive journalistic culture with potential for improving the quality of journalism. For these developments to take effect, newsrooms will constantly require new skills and training on a range of techniques and skills surrounding participatory journalism and UGC.

Overall, there is still far more to discover in this area. Numerous questions remain about how users participate in the news process, as well what we can glean from a close examination of the discourses churned out on the comment forums beyond simply looking at what the journalists say they do with user comments, as the present study has broadly attempted to do.

NOTES

1. This hesitancy is also noted elsewhere; in offering an overview of the transformation of participatory journalism through the lenses of user comments, Zvi Reich (2011) observes that "comments functions have been a product of trial and error" as media organisations tried to steer users to more traditional channels.
2. Vincent Kahiya, speaking at the launch of a new edition, the *Southern Eye*, by the AMH group (http://www.southerneye.co.zw/2013/05/31/ncube-speaks-on-southern-eye-launch/).
3. The state-controlled press in Zimbabwe is generally perceived to be blatantly partisan in its support for the Zimbabwe African National Union—Patriotic Front (ZANU-PF), which until the establishment of a power-sharing deal with the leading opposition political party, the Movement for Democratic Congress (MDC) in 2008, was the ruling party in Zimbabwe since independence in 1980.
4. It was, however, also clear that the newsrooms are still figuring out how to navigate and "normalise" the interactive and participatory culture into established day-to-day practices.
5. The Shona and Ndebele are two dominant ethnic groups in Zimbabwe.
6. Phunyukabemphethe is a penname derived from the local language (Ndebele), literally meaning slipping off from tight captivity. This offers a good example of the hidden identities on the comment forums.
7. See http://www.herald.co.zw/images/Terms_and_Conditions.pdf.
8. See "Important Notice to Our Readers" (http://www.newsday.co.zw/2013/06/24/important-notice-to-our-readers/).

REFERENCES

Accone, Tanya. 2000. "Digital Dividends for Journalism in Africa." *Nieman Reports.* 54 (4): 67–69.

Atton, Chris, and Hayes. M. Mabweazara. 2011. "New Media and Journalism Practice in Africa: An Agenda for Research." *Journalism: Theory, Practice & Criticism* 12 (6): 667–673.

Berger, Guy. 2005. "Powering African Newsrooms: Theorising How Southern African Journalists Make Use of ICTs for Newsgathering." In *Doing Digital Journalism: How Southern African Newsgatherers Are Using ICTs*, edited by Guy Berger, 1–14. Grahamstown: High Way Africa.

Bruns, Axel. 2008. "The Active Audience: Transforming Journalism from Gatekeeping to Gatewatching." In *News: the Ethnography of New Media Production Edited by Paterson, Chris and Domingo, David*, edited by Making. Online, 171–197. New York: Peter Lang.

Bruns, Alex, and Highfield, Tim. 2012. "Blogs, Twitter, and Breaking News: The Produsage of Citizen Journalism." In *Producing Theory in a Digital World: the Intersection of Audiences and Production in Contemporary Theory*, edited by Lind. A. Rebecca, 15–32. New York: Peter lang.

Canter, Lily. 2013. "The Misconception of Online Comment Threads: Content and Control on Local Newspaper Websites." *Journalism Practice* 7 (5): 604–619.

Deuze, Mark. 2003. "The Web and Its Journalisms: Considering the Consequences of Different Types of Newsmedia Online." *New Media & Society* 5 (2): 203–230.

Domingo, David. 2008. "Inventing Online Journalism: A Constructivist Approach to the Development of Online News." In *News: the Ethnography of New Media Production, Edited by Paterson, Chris and Domingo, David*, edited by Making. Online, 15–28. New York: Peter Lang.

Fenton, Natalie, and Witschge, Tamara. 2011. "Comment is Free, Facts Are Sacred: Journalistic Ethics in a Changing Mediascape." In *News Online: Transformation and Continuity*, edited by Graham and Redden Guy, Meikle, 148–163. Basingstoke: Palgrave Macmillan.

Frere, Marie Soleil. 2014. "Online Forums: How the Voices of Readers Are Reshaping the Sphere of Public Debate in Burkina Faso." In *Online Journalism in Africa: Trends, Practices and Emerging Cultures*, edited by Hayes. M. Mabweazara, Okoth. F. Mudhai and Whittaker, Jason, 237–258. London: Routledge.

Gulyas, Agnes. 2013. "The Influence of Professional Variables on Journalists' Uses and Views of Social Media." *Digital Journalism* 1 (2): 270–285.

Hermida, Alfred. 2011a. "Mechanisms of Participation: How Audience Options Shape the Coversation." In *Participatory Journalism: Guarding Open Gates at Online Newspapers*, edited by Singer, Jane, et. al., 13–33. New York: Wiley-Blackwell.

Hermida, Alfred. 2011b. "Fluid Spaces, Fluid Journalism: The Role of the 'Active Recipient' in Participatory Journalism." In *Participatory Journalism: Guarding Open Gates at Online Newspapers*, edited by Singer, Jane, et. al., 177–191. New York: Wiley-Blackwell.

Jensen, Klaus. B. 1982. "The Qualitative Research Process." In *A Hand Book of Media and Communication Research: Qualitative and Quantitative Methodologies*, edited by Jensen, Klaus B, 235–253. London: Routledge.

Lewis, Seth. C. 2012. "The Tension between Professional Control and Open Participation: Jornalism and Its Boundaries." *Information, Communication & Society* 15 (6): 836–866.

Mabweazara, Hayes. M. 2011. "Newsmaking Practices and Professionalism in the Zimbabwean Press." *Journalism Practice* 5 (1): 100–117.

Mabweazara, Hayes. M. 2013. "Normative Dilemmas and Issues for Zimbabwean Print Journalism in the 'Information Society' Era." *Digital Journalism* 1 (1): 135–151.

Mabweazara, Hayes. M. 2014. "Zimbabwe's Mainstream Press in the 'Social Media Age': Emerging Practices and Cultures." In *Online Journalism in Africa: Trends, Practices and Emerging Cultures*, edited by Mabweazara, Hayes M., Mudhai, Okoth F. and Whittaker, Jason, 65–86. London: Routledge.

Mabweazara, Hayes. M, Okoth. F. Mudhai, and Whittaker, Jason (eds.). 2014. *Online Journalism in Africa: Trends, Practices and Emerging Cultures*. London: Routledge.

Mason, Jennifer. 2006. *Qualitative Researching*. London: Sage.

McElroy Kathleen. 2013. "Where Old (Gatekeepers) Meets New (Media): Herding Reader Comments into Print" *Journalism Practice* 7 (6): 755–771.

Milioni, Dimitra. L, Vadratsikas Konstantinos, and Papa Venetia. 2012. "Their Two Cents Worth': Exploring User Agency in Readers." *Comments in Online News Media Observatorio* 6 (3): 21–47.

Moyo, Dumisani. 2009. "Citizen Journalism and the Parallel Market of Information in Zimbabwe's 2008 Elections." *Journalism Studies* 10 (4): 551–567.

Mudhai, Okoth, and F. 2004. "Researching the Impact of ICTs as Change Catalysts in Africa." *Ecquid Novi: South African Journal for Journalism Research* 25 (2): 313–335.

Pavlik, John. V. 2000. "The Impact of Technology on Journalism." *Journalism Studies*. 1 (2): 229–237.

Peters, Justin. 2011. "On Facebook and Freedom: Why Journalists Should Not Surrender to the Walmarts of the Web." *Columbia Journalism Review* 50 (4): 155–160.

Reich, Zvi. 2011. "User Comments: The Transformation of Participatory Space." In *Participatory Journalism: Guarding Open Gates at Online Newspapers*, edited by Singer Jane. B., et. al, 96–117. Malden MA: Wiley-Blackwell.

Santana, Arthur. D. 2011. "Online Readers' Comments Represent New Opinion Pipeline." *Newspaper Research Journal.* 32 (3): 66–81.

Sigal, Leon. V. 1973. *Reporters and Officals: The Organisation and Politics of News.* London: D.C. Heath and Company.

Singer, Jane. B. 2009. "Separate Spaces: Discourse about the 2007 Scottish Elections on a National Newspaper Website." *International Journal of Press/Politics* 14 (4): 477–496.

Singer, Jane. B., Alfred Hermida, David Domingo, Ari Heinonen, Steve Paulussen, Thorsten Quandt, Zvi Reich, and Marina Vujnovic. 2011. "Introduction: Sharing the Road." In *Participatory Journalism Guarding Open Gates at Online Newspapers*, edited by Singer, Jane et. al, 1–9. New York: Wiley-Blackwell.

Wimmer, Roger. D, and Dominick, Joseph. R. 2000. *Mass Media Research: An Introduction*. London: Wadsworth.

NEGOTIATING CONVERGENCE
"Alternative" journalism and institutional practices of Nigerian journalists

Motilola Olufenwa Akinfemisoye

This article critically interrogates the impact of new information and communication technologies on the institutional practices of mainstream journalists in Nigeria with particular reference to current newsroom practices and how user-generated content (UGC) was incorporated into mainstream media coverage of the 2011 Nigerian election. Rooted in the sociology of journalism, the study employs an ethnographic approach to examine the implications of new information and communication technologies for journalistic practices in Nigeria. With a reading of new information technologies as "alternative journalism", the ethnography, which deployed in-depth interviews with print journalists as well as newsroom observation, investigated whether "alternative journalism" is challenging traditional newsroom culture in Nigeria. The findings suggest that alternative journalism is redefining the roles of mainstream journalists as "news producers". Journalists have become "gatewatchers" with everyone else, especially during the 2011 elections when citizens actively engaged with alternative journalism in reporting the elections. However, mainstream journalists continue to contest their hegemonic traditional practices of giving prominence to "official" sources in news reporting, and negotiate how "alternative journalism" in the form of UGC is networked into mainstream reporting to avoid publishing rumours. The study concludes that contrary to scholarship that sees digital technologies as "de-professionalising" journalists, mainstream journalism in Nigeria maintains the dominant discourse by articulating and appropriating content from "alternative" sources for subtle economic motives.

Introduction

The proliferation of new digital technologies has heralded discourses about their potential to revolutionise many aspects of human existence and even leapfrog development for developing economies like those in Africa. This has witnessed calls for caution, with Alzouma (2005, 351) arguing that "the general conditions in which people are living do not change suddenly with the introduction of the internet". The impacts of these digital technologies on the speed at which information disseminates has also been said to impact on journalistic practices, making for a shift in the balance of power and blurring the lines between journalists and "the-people-formerly-known-as-the-audience" (Rosen 2006). The narrative is that the rise of the internet and mobile phones, among other new information and communication technologies, is transforming journalism, making it increasingly an "interactive practice" (Heinrich 2013), while journalists are becoming "robohacks" (Hargreaves 2003) who practise "churnalism" (Davies 2008). This appears to paint a picture of what is happening in "Western" mediaspheres. However, exploring whether (or not) the presence of these new digital technologies is influencing the institutional practices of professional journalists in Africa, and particularly Nigeria which is the focus in this article, is pertinent in order to identify not only how shifting journalistic cultures are emerging but also identify how Nigerian journalists are adapting to the digital revolution.

This study therefore interrogates whether (or not) the adoption of digital technologies in Nigerian newsrooms and the inclusion of user-generated content (UGC) in mainstream reporting are redefining the institutional journalistic practices of Nigerian journalists and creating "new" newsroom cultures. Drawing on an ethnographic approach, the study investigates how mainstream journalists adopt digital technologies and incorporate UGC in their daily journalistic routines, questioning if this is necessarily impacting on traditional journalistic structures in Nigeria. In examining these trends, the coverage of Nigeria's 2011 elections provides an example for benchmarking which, if any, new trends and cultures are emerging in Nigerian newsrooms with the adoption of new digital technologies.

Nigerian media have since their birth in 1859 been influential in the country's democratisation project, with the 1990s being particularly significant in its political history. Although the media "developed and crystallized along ethnic lines with underlying religious cum ethnic undertones" (Dare 2011, 12), it has remained "one of the most resilient and daring segments of Nigeria's civil society" (Olukotun 2004, 71) as well as one that "has had the most successful radical press in the democratisation struggle in Africa" (Adebanwi 2011, 48). The transition from military rule to civilian rule in 1999 did not come without a price as the freedom of Nigerian media was greatly hampered with the promulgation of draconian laws such as Decree 2 of 1984, the Nigerian Press Council Decree No. 85 of 1992, the Newspapers Decree No. 43 of 1993, and a host of others. Decree 2 of 1984, for instance, empowered the Inspector General of Police to detain indefinitely, without trial, any person considered as a risk to state security (see Ojebode 2011); many journalists were imprisoned and assassinated.[1] However, with the return to civil rule in 1999, the Nigerian press still grapples with being truly independent, with a recent press freedom index ranking placing it at 115th position out of 179 countries (Reporters Without Borders 2013).

With the widespread adoption of the World Wide Web and other digital technologies which continue to provide a breeding space for alternative journalistic practices to thrive (Atton 2013, 132), Nigerian journalism provides an excellent avenue for examining what the presence of "non-mainstream" journalism means for the institutional practices of journalists in "non-Western" mediaspheres. In examining this trend, the coverage of the elections of 2011 in Nigeria presents a useful illustration for probing how "alternative" journalisms are negotiating spaces within the mainstream media. "Alternative" media and "alternative" journalism(s), used interchangeably in this article, are defined following Atton and Couldry (2003, 579) as "media produced outside mainstream media institutions and networks".

The adoption of new information and communication technologies such as the internet, personal computers and mobile phones in Nigeria continues to witness a geometric progression with internet penetration, for instance, rising from 0.16 per cent in 2000 to about 29 per cent as at June 2012 (Miniwatts Marketing Group 2012). Mobile phones are also increasingly becoming ubiquitous in Africa and have recently been labelled as the "new talking drum of everyday Africa" (de Bruijn, Nyamnjoh, and Brinkman 2009). In Nigeria, mobile phone subscriptions continue to rise, with the latest figures at April 2013 suggesting over 145 million subscribers from the 266,461 subscribers in 2001 (Nigerian Communications Commission 2013). The media, moreover, do not exist in isolation of these transformations. As new digital technologies become widespread, journalism in Nigeria is adopting these technologies in news production and dissemination processes. For instance, all major national dailies in Nigeria have an online presence on social networking sites and operate functioning websites where online versions of their newspapers are published.

New media in Africa particularly has been said to play major roles in the democratisation projects of many countries despite the issue of limited access (Nyamnjoh 2005; Arntsen 2010). Dunisami Moyo's (2010) study of the Zimbabwean 2008 elections reveals, for instance, how new alternative media, especially mobile phones, can act as "monitors of democracy". The adoption of these digital technologies in Nigeria have played vital roles in connecting the "people-formerly-known-as-the-audience" with mainstream journalists in the coverage of key events such as the elections of 2011, the Occupy Nigeria protests of 2012, among others where the use of hashtags, for instance, has allowed journalists to keep track of unfolding events.

Contextualising Nigeria's 2011 Elections

In April 2011, Nigerians went to the polls for the fourth time since the dawn of civil rule which had lasted 12 years. After three widely decried previous elections in 1999, 2003 and 2007, the elections of 2011 were undoubtedly crucial to Nigeria's political history. Scholars generally agree that elections are essential to the survival of democracies (Adejumobi 2000) and, as Bratton (1998, 52) tells us, although "elections do not in themselves constitute a consolidated democracy … [they] remain fundamental, not only for installing democratic governments, but as a necessary requisite for broader democratic consolidation". However, several previous attempts at consolidating a democratic government in Nigeria proved abortive with the collapse of the first republic between 1960 and 1966, the second republic from 1979 to 1983 and the annulment of the generally acclaimed free and fair election of 12 June 1993 which would have been the third republic. The fourth republic, however, began with the elections of 1999 and the subsequent military handover to civilian rule on 29 May 1999. Since returning to civil rule in 1999, elections in Nigeria, as Omotola (2010, 535) argues, "have been one of the main problems of the democratization process". For instance, Tar and Zack-Williams (2007, 540) concluded after the study of the 2007 elections that "like all previous post-independence elections, the 2007 elections were full of controversies and widely condemned as fraudulent, violent and stage-managed by the outgoing president Olusegun Obasanjo".

As such, the discrepancies of previous elections saw many observers within and outside Nigeria closely monitoring the elections of 2011 both offline and online. Nigeria's 2011 three-tier polls—national assembly, presidential and gubernatorial—initially scheduled to be held on 2, 9 and 16 April, and postponed due to electoral materials arriving late, were held on 9, 16 and 26 April, respectively. Despite the post-election violence that was evident in some parts of Nigeria, several more positive, if not glowing, appraisals of the 2011 election were offered. For Akhaine (2011, 649), "a distinct blend of political will and patriotism, buttressed by meaningful contributions from citizens, the civil service and the military all came together to make Nigeria's 2011 elections a success story". The Commonwealth Observer Group also commented that the "April 2011 elections marked a genuine celebration of democracy in Africa's most populous country" (Commonwealth Observer Group 2011). Also significant was the way social media was deployed during the electioneering campaign by politicians as well as during the elections. President Goodluck Jonathan, for instance, adopted Facebook as a medium for "dialoguing" with Nigerians on 28 June 2010 and subsequently made his first announcement to contest in the presidential election on Facebook on 15 September 2010 (Adibe and Odoemelam 2012; Jonathan, Facebook post, 15 September 2011). This presaged the significant role of alternative media in the coverage of the elections of 2011.

Consequently, the coverage of Nigeria's 2011 elections provides an example for benchmarking the new trends and cultures which are emerging in Nigerian newsrooms with the proliferation of new information and communication technologies and mobile telephony, which made audience participation in reporting the 2011 elections unprecedented and remarkable. This study will further explore how the presence of "alternative" journalisms are impacting on the daily practices of Nigerian journalists and whether the appropriation of UGC into mainstream reporting is necessarily challenging their institutional practices.

Methodological Approach

In gathering empirical data for this study, an ethnographic approach comprising semi-structured interviews with professional journalists in Nigeria and a non-participant newsroom observation was adopted in investigating what new "alternative" media means for the institutional journalistic practices of Nigerian journalists. In addition to the ethnography, a textual analysis of news texts written during the election was conducted to provide a reading of how Nigerian journalists included (or excluded) alternative media content in the coverage of the elections of 2011. As Singer (2009, 191) notes, "Such triangulation increases confidence in the interpretation of findings [and] it is particularly useful for exploring the "why" as well as the "what" of a subject".

On the ethnography of newsrooms, Cottle (2007, 2) explains that deploying an ethnographic approach to studying media organisations "help[s] to reveal the constraints, contingencies and complexities 'at work'" as well as help in understanding "the production of the discourses 'at play' within news media representations". Born (2005, 15) concurs that ethnography is "a sharp tool for discerning not just the unifying features but the divisions, boundaries and conflicts of the society being studied". In Willig's (2013, 373) words, "newsroom ethnographies have enabled us to go straight to the heart of news organisations and show us how journalists go about their daily routines". Thus, ethnography of newsrooms brings to the fore the socio-cultural realities in the newsroom, and provides useful evidence in explaining whether or not the proliferation of digital technologies is rewriting and reshaping journalistic practices in

Nigeria. Newsroom ethnography provided insights into the workings and practices of journalists in the news production process and revealed that journalists continue to contest their hegemonic role as the watchdog for citizens.

This study focused on Nigerian newspapers which have, despite many challenges, remained "one of the most resilient and daring segments of Nigeria's civil society" (Olukotun 2004, 71). Nigeria has the largest press in Africa (Olukotun 2004) with over 100 newspapers and magazines, with most of them being private commercial ventures (BBC News 2012). The exact statistics for Nigerian newspapers' circulation and readership is unknown because "Nigerian newspapers … do not make such information available to the public" (Akingbulu and Bussiek 2010, 9). Four privately owned national dailies, which are relatively popular among the Nigerian reading public, were sampled for this study. Most newspaper organisations in Nigeria have their headquarters in Lagos, South-West Nigeria, and three of the four included in this study fall into this category. The newspapers are: *The Punch*, a family-owned media organisation with headquarters in Lagos; *Vanguard*, owned by Vanguard Media Limited with headquarters in Lagos and established by a journalist; and the *Guardian* owned by Guardian Newspapers Limited with headquarters in Lagos. The fourth, *Nigerian Tribune*, is Nigeria's oldest surviving private newspaper established by the first Premier of Nigeria's Western region, Chief Obafemi Awolowo, and is headquartered in Ibadan, a city in the South-West of Nigeria.

The ethnography, which was conducted between April 2012 and April 2013, involved about 125 journalists, whose identities remain anonymous in line with the ethical approval obtained for this study. The journalists interviewed were selected using purposive and snowball sampling, where journalists were asked who they thought it would be valuable to interview next. All participants in the study also use new digital technologies accessed either through their newsrooms or via personal mobiles or Blackberry smartphones or a combination of both. This was a necessary criterion for ensuring that those who actively use digital technologies in carrying out their duties took part in the study.

The interviews were conducted at various locations, including the newsrooms, editors' offices, and online journalists' offices[2] and the staff refectories. Included among the semi-structured interviews were questions about whether alternative journalistic practices were impacting on the way journalists carry out their institutional routine, how reports from alternative media sites were judged newsworthy and included in reporting the elections of 2011, and whether they agreed with notions that alternative media should be networked into the mainstream media. The interviews were transcribed, analysed and coded into themes.

Observations for this study occurred primarily in daily-section newsrooms of the four newspapers. Additional observation took place in the weekend newsroom of *Nigerian Tribune* and refectories of *The Punch* and *Vanguard*. Evidence that "African journalists have not shied away from exploiting digital technology in sourcing news and information" (Mudhai 2011, 681) was also gleaned from the observations since the mobile phone (and particularly Blackberry) was an evident and ubiquitous tool which journalists used in news sourcing (see also Mabweazara 2011). In the following sections, I explore emerging trends in the studied newsrooms and how mainstream journalists incorporated UGC in reporting the elections of 2011.

Covering Nigeria's 2011 Elections: UGC and Journalists' Dilemmas

Nigerian journalism, it has been argued, has played instrumental roles in the transition to civil rule (Agbese 2006; Dare 2011; Olukotun 2004), especially with the guerrilla journalism activities during the 1990s. However, with the influx of new information and communication technologies which made audience participation and engagement remarkable during the elections of 2011, mainstream journalists, according to one *Tribune* reporter, had to actively engage with "new" digital technologies in order to "be on top of information" from various polling stations:

> As journalists ..., we were asked to sign up for Facebook and Twitter accounts in the run-up to the elections so that we could easily monitor what people were posting on social media. But we still had to verify these stories because in Nigeria, people like to blow events out of proportion.

In reporting the elections of 2011, UGCs posted on various alternative media sites served as "leads" for the mainstream journalists who still had to verify such information from official sources. In the words of a senior journalist at *Tribune*:

> The trend during the election was that people posted different results. Ten people from the same polling station usually had varying reports but we had to wait for the official reports from INEC [Independent National Electoral Commission, Nigeria's electoral body] before we published such information.

The presence of election reports on alternative media sites also meant that Nigerian journalists did not necessarily have to be physically present at all the electoral polling stations to know what was happening. They could remain at their offices and act as "verifiers" and news aggregators:

> The activities of ordinary citizens who were tweeting from various polling stations, updating their Facebook pages as well as those who posted blog posts really augmented our roles as journalists. It helped widen the scope of our reports and gave it more depth, especially considering that there were many areas that we could not physically send a reporter to. We simply had to confirm and verify the stories from the official sources.

This comment reveals how the presence of alternative journalism is reshaping the practices of Nigerian journalism with regards to the pool of information sources available to draw from. It also signals how journalists sometimes resist including "alternative voices" while preferring to leave the *status quo* unchallenged.

For mainstream Nigerian journalists, reporting the elections of 2011 posed several challenges, especially with regards to obtaining comments on the true picture of events as the elections progressed because the official sources who ought to make such information available are "constantly seeking to control information flow for the benefit of the ruling elite" (Eti 2012, 24). The fear of libel suits and litigation is also a dilemma that mainstream journalists in Nigeria contend with when incorporating information from alternative media sites into their reports. A senior editor at *Tribune* explains:

> According to a law by the Federal government, we cannot publish election results until they have been confirmed by INEC. Although we had a lot of people sending us pictures of anomalies at various polling stations, we couldn't risk just publishing anything that was posted online. Being a registered corporate body we can be sued for misleading the public if we just go by whatever we find on alternative media platforms.

Issues of media ownership leading to journalists' adoption of self-censorship again influenced how mainstream Nigerian journalists appropriated reports from alternative media sites into their coverage of the elections of 2011. A journalist from *Vanguard* articulates how this challenge played out during the elections:

> Many people used their mobile phones to capture scenes of how the elections went in their constituencies. But there were some occasions where even after our colleague on the ground had verified such reports, our bosses advised against using the report because "you can't bite the finger that feeds you". This remains a serious challenge to our profession because even with the passing of the FOI Act[3] the sponsors and owners [of mainstream media] still determine what gets through.

This comment thus presents some of the issues Nigerian journalists contend with such as proprietorial interference that limits what journalists are allowed to report even when the data to support such reports are available. It also reveals that the adoption of new information and communication technologies in Nigerian newsrooms is localised based on the cultural context.

Notwithstanding the dilemmas which the presence of alternative journalism content posed for Nigerian journalists in the coverage of the elections of 2011, some of the newspapers solicited for UGC to be posted to a section of their websites dedicated to election monitoring. *Vanguard*'s online news report for 2 April 2011, the day that the elections were initially scheduled to begin, for example, had its headline as "Today's Election: What's Happening in Your Area?" *Vanguard* 2011. This is in direct contrast to what journalists traditionally do, in that instead of "reporting" the election, the news text goes on to say "Vanguard invites you to be part of today's history by telling the world what is happening in your area as Nigerians vote today". This direct invitation for the audience and other "writer-gatherers" (Couldry 2010), to become part of the news production process by "post[ing] news, photos and videos of elections or events they find interesting for the world to see at Vanguard's highly interactive community" bears testimony to the narrative that the proliferation of new digital technologies has made journalists become "gatewatchers" together with everyone else (Bruns 2008).

The Punch's online news text of 10 April 2011, the day after the start of the elections of 2011 which began with the national assembly election, opens with the headline "The Facebook, Twitter Election" (Ogunseye 2011). The most obvious part of this headline is its allegory. The previous day's national assembly election is here described not as a typical Nigerian election but as one where social media played defining roles. The election is also framed in this news text as though it was organised and carried out on social networking sites as the writer of the news text explained: "The tweets, Facebook updates, Skype messages and pictures that voters exchanged via emails and mobile phones gave [INEC] addresses of the polling booths, the locations, the number of people who … voted and the votes that each party won". The reporter further noted that *"while it is too early … to measure the role … the new media are likely to exert on the results…"* (emphasis added). Here, citizens' use of alternative media is celebrated as being responsible for tasks such as successful vote counting and other activities which constitutionally fall within the ambits of the electoral commission. Running through this text are direct quotes from alternative media sources which are used to create an impression of the mainstream's inclusion of "unofficial" news sources, thus revealing a smokescreen shift in the institutional practices of Nigerian journalism. As such, the power structures inherent within the text, with reference to choice of news sources, emphasise the audience as shaping the media agenda in this text. Ross (2007, 466) points out that "who is asked to speak in the news, as well as what the news is, says crucially important things about whose voice counts, who has status in the society".

However, the voices represented in the news texts analysed above might not necessarily be reflective of an inclusive media as market forces played critical roles in the ways UGC was incorporated into the Nigerian media's coverage of elections of 2011. Jodi Dean's concept of communicative capitalism which "designates that form of late capitalism in which values heralded as central to democracy take material form in networked communication technologies" (Dean 2008, 104), aptly captures the scenario that played out in the ways mainstream journalists appropriated UGC in reporting the elections of 2011. A senior editor at *Vanguard* explained:

> During the elections, we had a number of interactive reports on our website, and invited the audience to tell us what was going on in their areas. We did that deliberately because those are some of the stuffs that drive traffic to our website and advertisers will only advertise based on the value of the traffic. At the end of the day, the interaction between us and the audience was simply part of the "gizmo" [*sic*] to drive traffic to our website [and was not necessarily to voice the voiceless]. The in-thing during the elections was that everyone had something to say and we decided to hone in on that.

This raises a relevant point about how the economies of scale and the need for privately owned media organisations to remain afloat impact on the way UGC is appropriated in the mainstream media. These findings also reveal that despite UGC constituting a part of the mainstream media's coverage of the elections of 2011, the narrative that the "self-image [of journalists] has been thoroughly shaken", as Bogaerts and Carpentier (2013, 60) argue, might not necessarily be the case in Nigeria. Journalists in Nigeria generally see themselves as the "society's truth-teller[s]" (McNair 1998, 65). As the online news editor at the *Guardian* notes, "You still have to look out for newsworthy tweets and filter it out to report what is news. That's what we did during the elections".

Journalism-on-the-go: When the Present is the Deadline

Although technological convergence is evident in Nigerian newsrooms in that all the four media organisations visited had computers connected to the internet, other socio-economic implications are evident. Findings from this study reveal that journalists in Nigeria are not only adapting to the changes that the presence of "alternative" media sources in the form of UGC introduce, but are also competing with "alternative" media practitioners in being the first to break news. A senior editor at *The Punch* explained:

> Things are a lot more dynamic now and alternative media is really putting us on our toes in that we too want to be the first to break news. Sometimes we change our cover story up to four times before going to press because we want to be sure that we beat all our competitors to it. One of the greatest challenges facing us as journalists

> is that our profession is becoming "journalism-on-the-go"; producing restaurant-style food at the speed of flipping burgers at a fast-food joint. We are still serving the same menu but the timing is now very different if we are to remain relevant in these times. You can run a reaction to what has been trending on social media. The challenges that reporters grapple with are now much more complex than they used to be before.

This quote reveals some of the dilemmas which Nigerian journalists face with the presence of digital technologies, forcing them to embrace dynamism in order to remain sustainable. It also shows how journalists continue to contest their hegemonic presence as "the nation's social conscience", to use Olukotun's (2002, 318) words, in the face of other platforms which also provide newsworthy information.

Observations at newsrooms also revealed some emerging trends in the way Nigerian journalists practise their trade. Whereas traditionally journalists would go to their beats, follow up stories and in some cases contact the official sources relevant to the story via fixed lines or more recently via mobile phones (either through phone calls or text messages), the presence of alternative media sites has added another dimension to the news beats which Nigerian journalists visit as part of their daily routine. As was explained by a senior editor at the *Guardian*:

> When I get to the newsroom every day, I have a list of about five alternative media outlets whose websites I visit first thing in the morning as soon as I resume for the day to see what the buzz is. I check Sahara reporters, Premium times Nigeria, Huhuonline, Pointblank news and Elendu reports to see some of the stories they are following. These alternative media sites usually have scoops which I can then assign a reporter to work on during the day.

This again raises the point that the working routines of mainstream journalists are being reshaped by the presence of alternative media. Journalists now not only have to attend to their various news beats, but also have to monitor alternative media sites as both competitors and news-lead-providers, in a bid to produce newsworthy content as well as report what is happening off- and online.

For mainstream Nigerian journalists, the meaning of deadline and production time have changed drastically in that the presence of UGC, just clicks away, means that the present is the deadline. Rather than the traditional freedom of waiting 24 hours before a story is updated, mainstream journalists in Nigeria increasingly find themselves struggling to keep up with immediacy "because there is too much information online … so you have to zero in from a particular point" (reporter, *The Punch*).

Observations also showed that sports journalists gleaned more information from social networking sites, which have become new news beats, in writing their stories than journalists on other desks. From following sportsmen and women on Twitter to gleaning reports from other mainstream sports website, a sports reporter at *The Punch* explained:

> I depend on social media a lot in writing my stories and we have the advantage of packaging and making stories fuller. I follow most footballers on Twitter and set up Google alerts to monitor what the sportsmen, especially footballers, are saying. For instance, in covering [Peter] Odemwingie's saga at West Bromwich football club, I monitored his tweets to get his reactions. Most times, these footballers tweet what they think of the next game or why they didn't win a game *as such not being at my Twitter beat will mean missing a big story.* (emphasis added)

This finding reveals another emerging practice in Nigerian newsrooms where journalists do not necessarily have to physically interview news sources but can glean comments made on their social network pages and pass such on as news. While this practice may bridge the gap of access to some news sources, it might make journalists susceptible to publishing falsehood in instances where the source's online account has been hacked.

Alternative Journalism and Nigeria's Mainstream Media: Connecting the Dots

The presence of various alternative journalistic practices has led to calls that professional journalists and Rosen's (2006) people-formerly-known-as-the-audience, should collaborate in the news production process, fostering the idea of a networked media ecology. This study, however, revealed that mainstream Nigerian journalism regards alternative media practices as competition and would rather not collaborate in the ways networked journalism scholars advocate where "publics acting as creators, investigators, reactors, (re)makers and (re)distributors of news and where all variety of media, amateurs and professional, corporate and independent products and interests intersect at a new level" (Russell 2011, 1). The gates are still very high in Nigerian newsrooms, not only in terms of audience inclusion in reporting but also in terms of who is allowed on their premises. At *The Punch*, the news editor and other senior journalists had a closed-door management meeting which lasted almost three hours during the fieldwork for this study. The editor later briefed this researcher that they were discussing strategies of maximising their website to drive more useful traffic which advertisers will pay for. He also mentioned that they were becoming worried at the way some of their stories were published on alternative media sites and blogs without attribution.

Observation during this study revealed that some traditional structures remain. At the four newsrooms where ethnography for this study was conducted, some traditional practices remain. Editorial conferences, where about 7–10 senior editors came together to discuss the stories that made it to the pages of their competitors as well as typographical errors in the day's edition, were held daily. News story ideas which can be developed in future editions are also collaboratively discussed during these editorial conferences. This suggests that news production is still very much a collaborative effort in a bid to ensuring that all information published has been thoroughly verified.

So in spite of the activities of alternative media practitioners, mainstream media journalists in Nigeria still hold very strongly to their traditional institutional practices. A senior editor at *The Punch* explains:

> The presence of alternative journalism practices doesn't translate into more openness or press freedom. Government officials complain about how people use social media and, if they have their way, they would regulate freedom online. In recent times, for instance, top government officials complain about how people use social media and have called for censoring. We are always trying to be careful that in incorporating materials from alternative media sites, we don't become tools in the hands of rumour peddlers.

This reveals that the potential of alternative media for media democratisation in Nigeria has yet to be achieved. Being a country where many subtle interests are likely to be parts of the agenda of alternative media practitioners, mainstream journalists still exercise caution in incorporating reports from alternative sites.

Newsroom observation at *Vanguard* again revealed that institutional routines of breaking leaks to readers may not necessarily be eluding mainstream journalists in the wake of Assange's WikiLeaks. The following scenario offers an illustration:

> It's 1710 hrs. A scoop about explosives found buried in the house of a politician in Kaduna state [a Northern Nigerian state] has just come through via a Blackberry message. The deputy editor puts a call through from the Lagos headquarters to the mobile phone of the correspondent in Kaduna state asking him to verify the story and to send photographs of the site. The Kaduna correspondent had not heard about the story before the call from the deputy editor and promises to investigate. The newsroom becomes very rowdy and noisy as reporters who have gone out on assignments return to hand in their stories. The sub-desk reporters continue planning other pages, while the cover and page 3 await findings about the explosives. Other editors too make frantic calls to out-station correspondents to send in their stories so they can be approved and the pages planned. Frustration rises too especially when the editorial content for the next edition had not been approved by the editor. In the midst of this chaos, the deputy news editor remains on the phone to the correspondent in Kaduna and is monitoring other newspaper websites to see if they had posted any information about the explosives. The online editor is not permitted to share it as breaking news on the website yet. And the scoop paid off, only *Vanguard* had the story on its front page the following day. (Notes from newsroom observation at *Vanguard*, 6 March 2013)

These findings show that in spite of the exposés which alternative media break, mainstream journalists still stick to their professional journalistic routines of fact-checking and verification before publishing stories. Evidence from the observations also revealed emerging news cultures where UGC is appropriated to become part of the mainstream. For instance, at the time of the researcher's fieldwork at *The Punch* newspaper, the organisation had six weeks earlier launched a new page in its print edition called *i-punch* where latest trends on social media were reported and the reactions of selected Nigerians got published. The *Punch* reporter in charge of this page noted that "alternative media in Nigeria is a competition and *the mainstream media too had to keep up with that challenge*" (emphasis added). Asked whether alternative media is redefining journalism practices in Nigeria, a senior editor noted:

> Alternative media have only come to complement the existing structures in Nigerian media. There's still this traditional attachment to newspapers in Nigeria. Nigerians still have the attachment to printed matter and some advertisers still prefer to advertise in physical newspapers. Alternative media has also provided the means for us as journalists to uphold the integrity of our reportage because people still want to check that what they have read on alternative media platforms is the truth.

Although mainstream journalists in Nigeria claim to "uphold integrity in [their] reportage", issues of self-censorship remain an impediment to being the society's watchdog. A reporter at *Vanguard* commented on the challenge journalists in Nigeria face in terms of being restricted on what they can report:

> Most funding come from the corridors of power and *you cannot afford to bite the finger that feeds you*. No media organisation in Nigeria can claim to survive on circulation funds because the bulk of adverts still come from the government. As such, even when there are reports on alternative media about the government, which may be true, we still apply self-censorship because we can be sued for using such stories. (emphasis added)

Market forces make for self-censorship on the part of the journalists and the poor remuneration of journalists, as Mabweazara's (2010) study of Zimbabwean journalists revealed, is also prevalent in Nigeria. In the words of Oso (2012, 33) this has "seriously whittled down any form of commitment to professionalism among journalists. It has also made the news making process so porous that it is very easy for parochial interests in political society to penetrate the news columns".

Conclusion

This study has shown that the permeation of new information and communication technologies as well as the presence of alternative journalisms in Nigeria may not necessarily be re-wiring journalistic structures in Nigeria. However, the institutional practices of mainstream journalists are being challenged. Since hegemony is never complete, journalists continue to contest their space in the mediascape by going beyond just breaking news to providing more in-depth and interpretive reports. As was the case during the elections of 2011, Nigerian journalists sought out ways to maximise profits in the ways they incorporated UGC into their coverage of the elections. As such, the presence of alternative journalisms is making mainstream Nigerian journalism rethink its business models.

In the words of an assistant news editor at *The Punch*, "we are maximising all platforms so that we will still remain sustainable in the face of alternative media". Despite the availability of the internet and computers in all the newsrooms sampled for this study, Nigerian journalists still hold on to their traditional structures of holding editorial conferences where every participant was physically present. Although journalists are increasingly adapting UGC to mainstream reporting, these inclusions were mostly negotiated to suit the interests of the media organisations as well as fit into established news-making practices.

Another key finding of this study is the centrality of local context factors in shaping and constraining how UGC is appropriated in the newsrooms studied. Issues of proprietorial interference, for instance, has led to a culture of censoring discourses from alternative media sources in order to avoid slighting advertisers and funding which mostly comes from the corridors of power.

This study concludes that despite dominant narratives suggesting mainstream journalism faces extinction with the presence of digital technologies which fuel alternative media, Nigeria's mainstream media is adapting to these changes by appropriating these supposed threats to economic advantage.

ACKNOWLEDGEMENT

The author acknowledges the comments of George Ogola of the School of Journalism and Digital Communication, University of Central Lancashire as well as that of the two anonymous reviewers.

NOTES

1. Nduka Irabor and Tunde Thompson were two print journalists working for the *Guardian* newspaper who were imprisoned during Muhammadu Buhari's regime in 1984 for publishing an investigation about missing funds in the petroleum ministry (Ojebode 2011).
2. The journalists in charge of the newspapers' websites at *The Punch* and *Guardian* had their desks in separate offices from the newsroom. This I was told during one of the interviews, was to "facilitate better concentration" in monitoring alternative media sites (online journalist, *Guardian*).
3. Nigeria's Freedom of Information Act was passed into law in 2011.

REFERENCES

Adebanwi, Wale. 2011. "The Radical Press and Security Agencies in Nigeria: Beyond Hegemonic Polarities." *African Studies Review* 54 (3): 45–69.

Adejumobi, Said. 2000. "Elections in Africa: A fading Shadow of Democracy?" *International Political Science Review* 21 (1): 59–73.

Adibe, Kenneth N., and Chinedu Odoemelam. 2012. "Social Media, Electioneering and Sustenance of Democracy in Africa: A "SWOT." *Analysis Africa Media & Democracy Journal* 1 (1). http://www.amdmcjournal.net/pdf/14swot.pdf

Agbese, Aje-Ori. 2006. *The Role of the Press and Communication Technology in Democratisation: The Nigerian story*. New York & London: Routledge.

Akhaine, Sylvester O. 2011. "Nigeria's 2011 Elections: The 'Crippled Giant' Learns to Walk?" *African Affairs* 110 (441): 649–655.

Akingbulu, Akin, and Hendrik Bussiek. 2010. "Nigeria: A survey by the Africa Governance Monitoring and Advocacy Project (AfriMAP), Open Society Initiative for West Africa (OSIWA), Open Society Media Program (OSMP)." *Open Society Foundations*. Available at http://www.afrimap.org/english/images/report/AfriMAP_Nigeria_Broadcasting_2011.pdf

Alzouma, Gado. 2005. "Myths of Digital Technology in Africa: Leapfrogging Development?" *Global Media and Communication* 1 (3): 339–356.

Arntsen, Hilde. 2010. "Committing Journalism? A view of the Zimbabwean 2008 General Elections as interpreted by Internet news cartoons." *Communicare Journal for Communication Sciences in Southern Africa* 29 (special edition): 18–41.

Atton, Chris. 2013. "Separate, Supplementary Or Seamless? Alternative News and Professional Journalism." In *Rethinking Journalism: Trust and Participation in a Transformed News Landscape*, edited by Chris Peters and Marcel Broersma, 131–143. London and New York: Routledge.

Atton, Chris, and Nick Couldry. 2003. "Introduction to Special Issue on Alternative Media." *Media, Culture & Society* 25 (5): 579–586.

BBC News. 2012. "Nigeria Profile." 26 July. Available at http://www.bbc.co.uk/news/world-africa-13949549

Bogaerts, Jo, and Nico Carpentier. 2013. "The Postmodern Challenge to Journalism." In *Rethinking Journalism: Trust and Participation in a Transformed News Landscape*, edited by Chris Peters and Marcel Broersma, 60–71. London and New York: Routledge.

Born, Georgina. 2005. *Uncertain Vision: Birt Dyke and the Reinvention of the BBC*. London: Vintage.

Bratton, Michael. 1998. "Second Elections in Africa." *Journal of Democracy* 9 (3): 51–66.

Bruns, Axel. 2008. "The Active Audience: Transforming Journalism from Gatekeeping to Gatewatching." In *Making Online News: The Ethnography of New Media production*, edited by Chris Paterson and David Domingo, 171–184. New York: Peter Lang.

Commonwealth Observer Group. 2011. "Nigerian Elections Interim Statement." accessed November 20, 2011, http://www.thecommonwealth.org/document/181889/34293/235960/2011_nigerian_elections_interim_statement.htm.

Cottle, Simon. 2007. "Ethnography and News Production: New(s) Developments in the Field." *Sociology Compass* 1 (1): 1–16.

Couldry, Nick. 2010. "New Online News Sources and Writer-Gatherers." In *New Media, Old News: Journalism and Democracy in the Digital Age*, edited by Natalie Fenton, 138–152. London: Sage.

Dare, Sunday. 2011. "The Rise of Citizen Journalism in Nigeria—A Case Study of Sahara Reporters." *Reuters Institute Fellowship Paper*: 1-74-Reuters Institute for the study of journalism.

Davies, Nick. 2008. *Flat Earth News: An Award-Winning Reporter Exposes Falsehood, Distortion and Propaganda in the Global Media*. London: Chatto & Windus.

De Bruijn, Mirjam, Francis B. Nyamnjoh, and Inge Brinkman. 2009. *Mobile Phones: The New Talking Drums of Everyday Africa*. Barmenda/Leiden: Langaa & Africa Studies Centre.

Dean, Jodi. 2008. "Communicative Capitalism: Circulation and the Foreclosure of Politics." In *Digital Media and Democracy*, edited by Megan Boler. Cambridge, MA: MIT Press.

Eti, Chigozi. 2012. "Deconstructing the Reporting of Hostage Taking in the Niger Delta." *Global Media Journal (African Edition)* 6 (1): 23–42.

Hargreaves, Ian. 2003. *Journalism: Truth or Dare*. Oxford University Press: Oxford and New York.

Heinrich, Ansgard. 2013. "News Making as an Interactive Practice: Global News Exchange and Network Journalism." In *Rethinking Journalism: Trust and Participation in a Transformed News Landscape*, edited by Chris Peters and Marcel Broersma, 89–100. London and New York: Routledge.

Mabweazara, Hayes M. 2010. "When Your 'Take-Home' Can Hardly Take You Home: Moonlighting and the Quest for Economic Survival in the Zimbabwean Press." *African Communication Research* 3 (3): 431–450.

Mabweazara, Hayes M. 2011. "The Internet in the Print Newsroom: Trends, Practices and Emerging Cultures in Zimbabwe." In *Making Online News: Newsroom Ethnographies in the Second Decade of Internet Journalism*, edited by David Domingo and Chris Paterson. 57–59New York: Peter Lang.

McNair, Brian. 1998. *The Sociology of Journalism*. London, New York, Sydney, Auckland: Arnold.

Miniwatts Marketing Group. 2012. "Internet Usage Statistics for Africa.", available from http://www.internetworldstats.com/stats1.htm accessed 30/02/2012

Moyo, Dunisami. 2010. "The New media as Monitors of Democracy: Mobile Phones and Zimbabwe's 2008 election." *Communicare Journal for Communication Sciences in Southern Africa* 29 (special edition): 71–85.

Mudhai, Okoth. F. 2011. "Immediacy and Openness in a Digital Africa: Networked-Convergent Journalisms in Kenya." *Journalism: Theory, Practice & Criticism* 12 (6): 674–691.

Nigerian Communications Commission. "Monthly Subscriber Data", accessed 11 June, 2013, http://www.ncc.gov.ng/index.php?option=com_content&view=article&id=125&Itemid=73.

Nyamnjoh, Francis. 2005. *Africa's Media: Democracy and the Politics of Belonging*. London: Zed Books.

Ogunseye, Toyosi. 2011. "The Facebook, Twitter Election." The Punch. http://archive.punchng.com/Articl.aspx?theartic=Art20110410230461 5. Accessed 20 November 2011.

Ojebode, Ayobami. 2011. "Nigerian Freedom of Information Act: Provisions, Strengths and Challenges." *African Communication Research* 4 (2): 267–284.

Olukotun, Ayo. 2002. "Authoritarian State, Crisis of Democratisation and the Underground Media in Nigeria." *African Affairs* 101: 317–342.

Olukotun, Ayo. 2004. "Media Accountability and Democracy in Nigeria, 1999-2003." *African Studies Review* 47 (3): 69–90.

Omotola, J. Shola. 2010. "Elections and Democratic Transition in Nigeria Under the Fourth Republic." *African Affairs* 109 (437): 535–553.

Oso, Lai. 2012. "Press and Politics in Nigeria: On Whose Side?" http://lasu.edu.ng/news/Press_and_Politics_in_Nigeria.pdf

Reporters without Borders. 2013. "Press Freedom Index 2013." Available at http://en.rsf.org/press-freedom-index-2013,1054.html. Accessed 30 May 2013.

Rosen, Jay. 2006. "The People Formerly Known as the Audience." Pressthink. Available at: http://archive.pressthink.org/2006/06/27/ppl_frmr.html

Ross, Karen. 2007. "The Journalist, the Housewife, the Citizen and the Press Women and Men as Sources in Local News Narratives." *Journalism: Theory, Practice & Criticism* 8 (4): 449–473.

Russell, Adrienne. 2011. *Networked: A contemporary History of News in Transition*. Cambridge: Polity.

Singer, Jane. 2009. "Ethnography." *Journalism & Mass Communication Quaterly* 86 (1): 191–198.

Tar, Usman, and Alfred B. Zack-Williams. 2007. "Nigeria: Contested Elections & An Unstable Democracy." *Review of African Political Economy* 34 (113): 540–548.

Vanguard Newspaper. "Today's Election: What's Happening in Your Area." Last modified April 2, accessed November 20, 2011, http://www.vanguardngr.com/2011/04/today%E2%80%99s-election-what%E2%80%99s-happening-in-your-area/.

Willig, Ida. 2013. "Newsroom Ethnography in a Field Perspective." *Journalism: Theory, Practice & Criticism* 14 (3): 372–387.

THE USE OF INFORMATION AND COMMUNICATION TECHNOLOGIES IN THREE EGYPTIAN NEWSROOMS

Ahmed El Gody

The basis of the information revolution in Egypt centres on the use and appropriation of technological advancements. At its forefront is the growth of information and communication technologies (ICTs), which offer an active and interactive platform for socio-political development, including the circumstances leading to the "25 January 2011 revolution", predominantly labelled as the "Facebook" or Twitter revolution'. After this "digital" revolution many Egyptians continued using cyberspace. They clustered in networks, created parallel communication systems, each with its own identity, and interacted on issues of common concern. Witnessing a changing environment, the Egyptian journalism industry has had no choice but to overcome its fear of adopting technologies in order to fit into the new mould. Several newsrooms have adopted ICTs in the hope that the new media would help them to develop their content and reconnect with their audiences. Although on the surface this implies development, this claim requires further assessment. This study therefore aims to investigate the implementation and appropriation of ICTs, especially internet technologies, in three Egyptian newsrooms: Al Ahram, Al Dostor, *and* Al Masry Al Youm. *The study further examines the extent to which newsrooms are incorporating ICTs into their daily routine as well as how the technologies are shaping and redefining practices.*

Introduction and Methodology

With the Egyptian society moving into the electronic age, more people are communicating in cyberspace not only to access information, but also to create "realities" of their own. Although these developments are virtual, they have proved that they can cross boundaries to the real world (El Gody 2012; Parks 2005). Since 2000 the number of internet users in Egypt has increased sevenfold, reaching 32.6 million by 2013 with 32.9 per cent penetration and a 38 per cent annual increase in high-speed internet subscribers. In 2013 mobile subscribers reached 96.1 million with 109.3 per cent penetration (Ministry of Communication and Information Technology 2013).

From 2006 Egyptians have been using information and communication technologies (ICTs) to debate current events, criticise the government, public officials and political parties, share personal experiences, propose solutions to current socio-political problems, and construct various visions of the country's future (El Gody 2007; Parks 2005). Citizens have been quick to harness ICTs, creating online news sites, blogs, video blogs, YouTube posts, podcasts, SMS text messages and mobile phone Web publishing, and establishing accounts on social networks like Facebook and Twitter. This has led to the production and dissemination of citizen-driven journalism and advocacy at a faster pace than the government can control, regulate or censor (El Gody 2014; Hamdy 2008; Salma 2009). Pintak (2010, 299) counted 13,500 active citizen news journalism websites in Egypt that provided "politically driven reportage on local events ... break[ing] numerous off-limits to the mainstream Egyptian media" by using ICTs and thus clustering citizens around the idea of embracing democratic change, ultimately paving the road to the 25 January 2011 revolution. ICTs, therefore, are seen as a tool to "empower" the Egyptian public to think of and develop programmes that respond to their specific needs.

Egyptian mainstream journalism seems to be far away from that approach (Murphy 2010) as it has been shaped by loyalty to the political regime for the past 60 years. One can thus use Rugh's (1979) classification of media in Egypt as being authoritarian. In this sense, the January 2011 political revolution did not change the Egyptian print media landscape (Freedom House 2012). Newspapers still appear bent on promoting the main political, social and economic programmes of the regime. The government steers the media agenda and the direction of news to filter what audiences hear and see. Egyptian journalists do not explore issues beyond the limits of the traditional connections and relationships between the political class and the rest of the population (El Gody 2005; Rugh 2004). The failure of the print media to have an active presence in people's lives has led the audience to turn to alternative, online, and independent media forms for news (Salama 2009).

Internet technology was introduced into Egyptian newsrooms in 1996 as a government-induced aid for media organisations to develop their new media infrastructure. The Dar Al Tahrir publication *Al Gomhuria* was the first Egyptian print newspaper to go online, using GIF/JPG images of clips from the newspaper. Between 1996 and 2000, 18 Egyptian newspapers, including the major dailies, joined the cyber world (El Gody 2012). By 2012, 69 publications, representing 49.8 per cent of the Egyptian print media industry, had their own websites (Information and Decision Support Center 2010; El Gody 2014). Although, superficially, this trend implies development, the question of whether ICTs have been realised and used in the daily routine of Egyptian newsrooms remains unanswered.

In this study, the term ICTs is used as an overarching expression covering all technical means of processing and communicating information. This term has gained popularity due to the convergence of information technologies and telecommunication technologies in journalism production. ICTs in newsrooms, therefore, comprise a broad range of integration and use of such technologies as computer hardware and software, the internet and internet technologies, networks, databases, television and radio satellite systems, multimedia, video, DVDs, and fixed and mobile telephones in daily journalism routines (Grossman and Helpman 2005; Singer 2006).

Writing about Egyptian journalists' uses of technology to communicate with their audience, Salama (2009) observes that while journalists pretend to know their audience —through technologies—and to generate "institutional knowledge", they are not using the technology to address citizens' needs or be part of their discussions. In transitional societies moving towards democracy, such as Egypt, political development is a central topic, which journalists mediate. Indeed, journalists inform the audience and facilitate informed choices as "gatewatchers", not as "gatekeepers" (Bruns 2005), in the power struggle between the audience, media, and politics. Egyptian journalists have been criticised for a number of things, including not being "connected" with their local audiences, for losing their ability to help citizens connect their everyday life with politics, and for failing in their capacity to encourage local people to participate in political debates or even to provide them with the skills needed for this participation (Burns 2005; El Gody 2012; Eliasoph 1998). However, when one turns to newspapers, the adoption and use of ICTs looks even more modest.

Against this backdrop, this study aims to explore the use of ICTs in daily news production. It examines the extent to which journalists integrate new media technologies into their work routines, as well as how journalists/news organisations interact with their audiences. Such understanding could assist the Egyptian print media to shift towards the Egyptian "network society".

To study the appropriation of new digital technologies by Egyptian newsrooms (pro-government *Al Ahram*, independent online *Al Dostor*,[1] and independent *Al Masry Al Youm*), this study has integrated qualitative ethnographic participant observation and structured and semi-structured interviews with a quantitative survey. The researcher spent 209 hours in the three newsrooms, with 82 hours spent with *Al Masry Al Youm*, 61 hours with *Al Dostor*, and 66 hours with *Al Ahram*. Observations were conducted in three waves in 2008, 2009, and 2011, in addition to personal interviews with 37 journalists/editors, to construct the ethnographic element of the study. Furthermore, two survey questionnaires in 2009 and 2011 comprised the quantitative section for this study. A total of 240 journalists (125 respondents participated in the 2009 survey tier—58 from *Al Ahram*, 34 from *Al Masry Al Youm*, and 33 from *Al Dostor*;115 respondents participated in the 2011 survey tier—59 from *Al Ahram*, 35 from *Al Masry Al Youm*, and 21 from *Al Dostor*) responded to the questionnaire, including 65 respondents who participated in both tiers. The overall statistical results reflect a proper sample from the three newsrooms under study with an average 43.9 per cent response. A non-probability purposive sample of journalists, editors, editors-in-chief, webmasters, online editors, and consultants were drawn. Different techniques were implemented in order to obtain the sample, including snowball, telephone calls, and face-to-face surveys.

Descriptive statistics using SPSS version 15.0 were used to analyse the data and to answer the questions. Data were analysed using frequency, distributions, percentages, means, and standard deviations. Cross-comparisons were also made between different organisations, stakeholders, genders, positions, and ownership.

Integrating quantitative and qualitative methods can be a useful method when conducting newsroom studies, especially in dealing with the integration of new media in news routines (Domingo 2006). The reasoning and justification are straightforward: it allows access to different levels and aspects within the scope of the study. Furthermore, because qualitative research and quantitative research have their own strengths and weaknesses, it is not hard to see that some issues would be relevant to one but not to the other (Bryman 2004).

Findings of the Study

Many factors determine the degree of adoption of different elements of ICTs in Egyptian newsrooms, including organisation ownership, economy, competition, management structure, editorial policy, and journalists' attitudes towards different technologies. In general, the media are controlled by the regulatory frameworks and policies of the country. This political and legal atmosphere, together with many economic factors, influence reporting techniques and limit the performance of journalism. Although Egypt has undergone socio-political changes that foster the democratisation process, in many ways the country's media still use traditional techniques that detach them from society's development goals. The following sections discuss the findings of the study, beginning with a close look at the ICT infrastructure and the setup of the three newsrooms under study.

ICT Infrastructure at Al Ahram

In 1994, *Al Ahram* became the first Egyptian newspaper to receive an internet connection. For *Al Ahram* management, the internet was seen as a tool to help document and verify already known facts and sources. This explains why internet connectivity was limited to the organisation's archive department located next to the editors' offices (see Figure 1). With the increase of the internet's popularity among journalists and their pressure to connect the newsroom, as well as increased internet connectivity in other Egyptian news organisations, *Al Ahram* management allowed internet connectivity first outside the newsroom, in the journalists' lounge on the 10th floor of the organisation. The internet was introduced inside the newsroom in 2001, with the change of wire service delivery to a standard online reception. However, management allowed internet connection partly inside the newsroom within the editors' section (see Figure 1). Internet connectivity was restricted to four workstations, called the "computer section", under the editors' supervision in order to make sure that journalists only used the technology within "limits of *Al Ahram*'s policy" that follows traditional newsroom power structure. Thus, computers with internet access were made available in the journalists' lounge room, where journalists used a "booking sheet" to access the internet. These computers are always busy with journalists "striving to do their work" (Ahmed Salem, personal communication, 2012; details of the interviewees are given in Appendix A). Inside the newsroom, journalists have access to computers with the internet for only a few minutes, "just to pull and verify information" (Moataz Aziz, personal communication, 2012).

Theoretically, the *Al Ahram* is properly wired (see Figure 2), but the internet has not been upgraded since 2005 even though the organisation receives its internet service from the government. High-speed internet is only allowed in high-managerial and editors' offices, thus clearly demonstrating how the adoption of new technologies in the newsroom is shaped by established power structures. The internet service inside the organisation is heavily censored and access to social media and other websites deemed "unnecessary" is banned. Internet technology services are maintained through the Ahram Management and Computer Centre (AMAC), which conducts a high level of surveillance over internet access, as well as over the organisation's email system. For this reason, *Al Ahram* journalists prefer using commercial email rather than the organisation's email system in order to escape organisational pressure and censorship. Wireless internet access is not permitted inside the organisation (Adel El Tohaiby, personal communication, 2009). This scenario echoes similar concerns elsewhere in

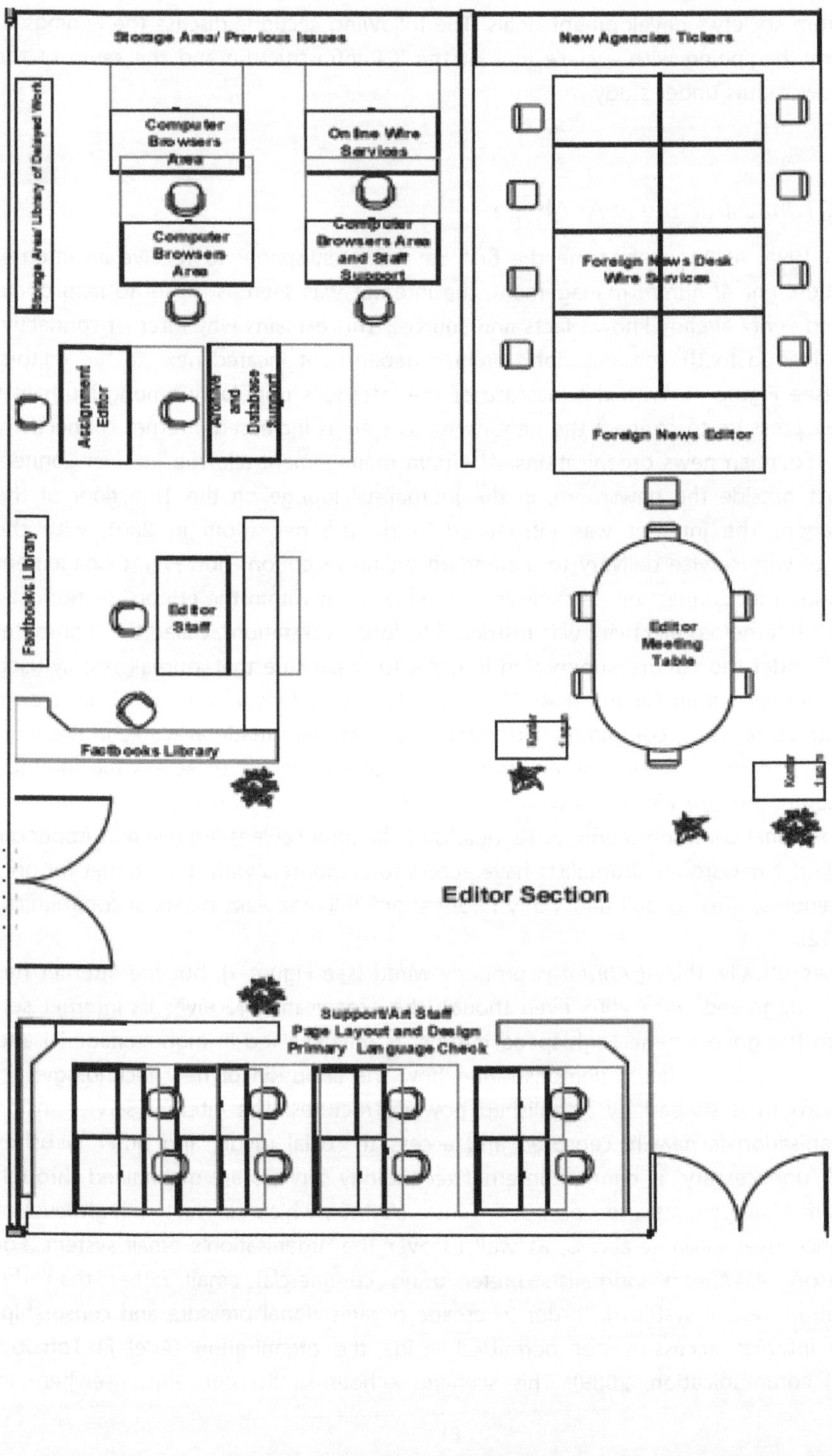

FIGURE 1
ICT infrastructure inside the *Al Ahram* newsroom

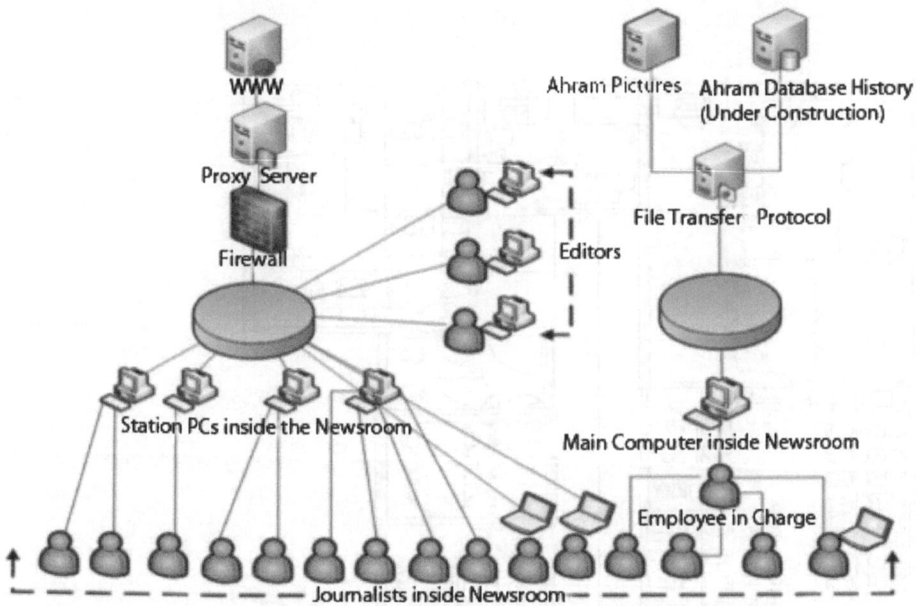

FIGURE 2
Al Ahram newsroom computer/internet networking system

Africa. For example, Skjerdal (2014, 99) writes about how security agents are "susceptible to tap [journalists'] personal email communication" in Ethiopian newsrooms. Similarly, Mabweazara (2011, 67) points to the ambivalences and fears associated with the use of email in Zimbabwean mainstream newsrooms as a result of "management's use of spyware to monitor and track email traffic".

The newsroom is also beset by a number of difficulties connected to limited and ageing technologies that are in dire need of upgrading. As the Online Editor and Multimedia Project Manager, Sameh Abdallah, put it "The computer system inside the organisation needs a real upgrade". In the same way, the number of personal computers in the newsroom is inadequate, with just "one computer for every 15–20 journalists". From observations in the newsroom one could easily see that the computers were old and slow, an observation that was confirmed by a number of journalists during interviews. The computers are regularly "down because they are not good brands and are way too old and over used". Another journalist in the newsroom stated: "management does not invest in purchasing good brands of computers or software programs … instead money is spent on painting the entrance to the building and upgrading 'editors' offices' rather than technological infrastructure". *Al Ahram* staff members were not encouraged to bring their own laptops into their workplace. Even if they do bring in a laptop, there is no printing facility for their work and limited internet cables to share, supposedly due to the necessity to maintain the bandwidth speed so it does not get overloaded. The layout and design computer is an Apple Macintosh G4[2] on which Al Nasher Al Sahafi, an Arabic-specialist program for publishing, is installed. These setbacks point to the pervasive nature of the "digital divide" and, in this sense, *Al Ahram* represents a typical African news organisation that is plagued by numerous digital divides of a technological, economic, and social nature.

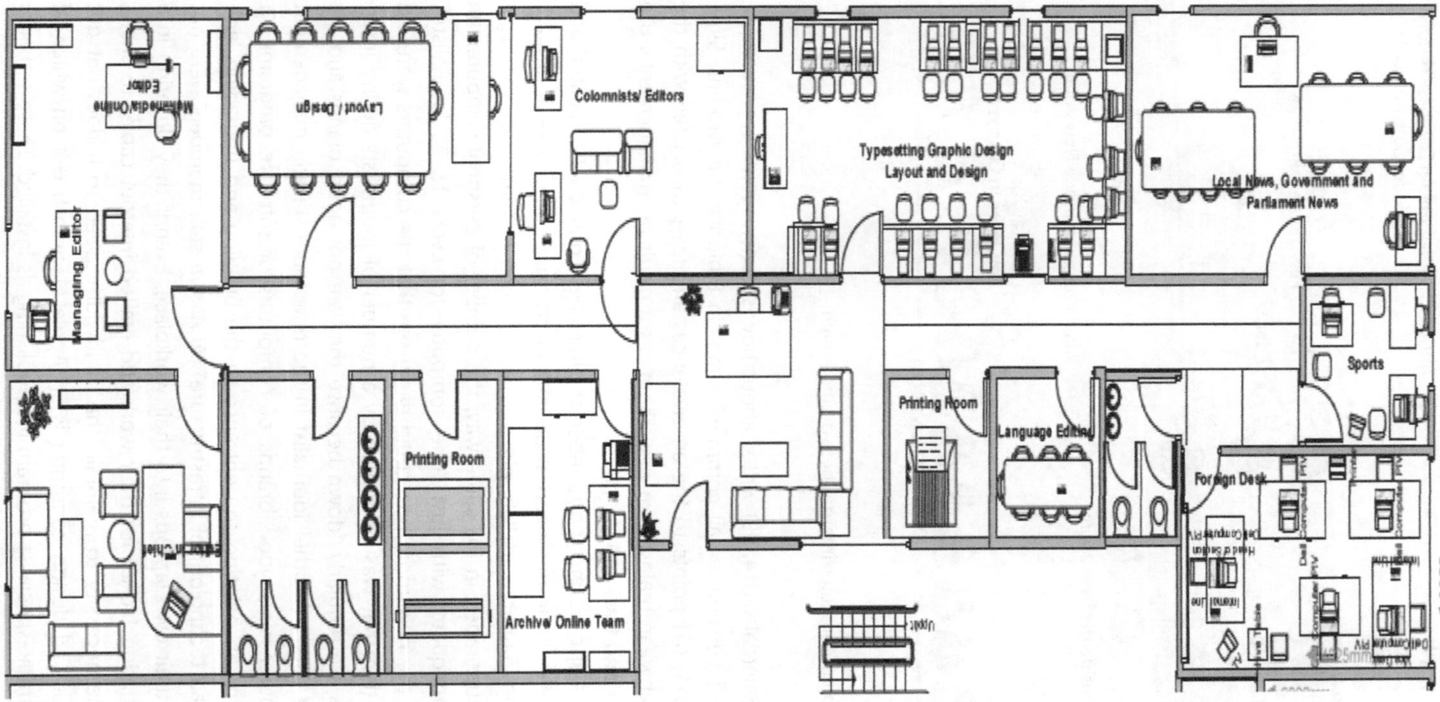

FIGURE 3
ICT map of the *Al Dostor* newsrocm

The AMAC is also responsible for the creation of the *Al Ahram* intra-network portal, which hosts the *Al Ahram* website, various *Al Ahram* publication websites, the email system, and the database. *Al Ahram* is the owner of ahram.org.eg and its mirrors ahram.com and ahram.co.uk, so it is not mistaken for other newspapers in the Arab world with the same name. Within the *Al Ahram* ownership package is the *Al Ahram* email system (@ahram.org and @ahram.org.eg). The organisation offers email to its management, editorial board, senior writers, and a number of "trusted" journalists. The majority of journalists are not offered organisational email addresses, fearing they could use *Al Ahram*'s name to conduct personal reporting for other publications; this also explains, as noted earlier, why members of the *Al Ahram* newspaper use commercial email. The email system is also hosted via the *Al Ahram* intranet work portal.

Al Ahram also maintains a simple database which has stored archived files since July 1998. Journalists and readers can retrieve past issues by searching for the date; however, they cannot search the dataset using keywords. The organisation has an intranet "system" to transfer files from the newsroom to the layout department and to send pictures from the archive to the newsroom and to the layout department.

In addition to the above, *Al Ahram* spent EGP 12,000,000 (US$1.6 million) on creating its photo-database. "This is our success story", stated Mr Nesseem Adel, Vice Editor of *Al Ahram*. The organisation owns one of the most valuable photo-documentation databases in Egyptian media, with over 14 million photos added since the early 1900s. To keep this "image treasure", AMAC launched a project in which all pictures are scanned, properly documented, and stored in the archive library. A computerised archive room was established where pictures from news agencies were filed in the system. Access to the photo-database is restricted to a few library personnel. Journalists who need archived pictures go to the library and browse the database with the librarian to choose the required picture. The picture is then transferred via the intranet work portal to the newsroom, to be observed by the journalist and editor on the "archive" computer run by another library staff member, which can then be approved and sent for layout. AMAC is working on the development of "an ambitious programme" where *Al Ahram* documents, including past issues, can be scanned and archived.

Given its "closed" and centralised newsroom system, and also for financial reasons—especially after the well-documented revolution—*Al Ahram* does not offer mobiles, laptops, or other forms of technologies to its employees. However, through the Egyptian Journalism Syndicate,[3] *Al Ahram* journalists are provided with special offers on laptops and special rates on mobile phone lines and equipment to encourage them to use the technology. The journalists' union inside *Al Ahram* provides such a service, but on a limited basis.

The *Al Ahram* newsroom is equipped with six television sets located next to the editor's section. The TV sets are hooked up to satellite receivers, which are programmed only to receive "pro-government" news channels. As one reporter explained, the televisions operate when "major events take place and need to be seen".

Fixed-line telephones remain a common feature in the newsroom. Fifty-seven landline telephones were counted inside the journalist section. Accessing internal lines can be done directly; however, accessing outside lines is done through dialling an external number. Accessing mobile phone lines requires a special request.

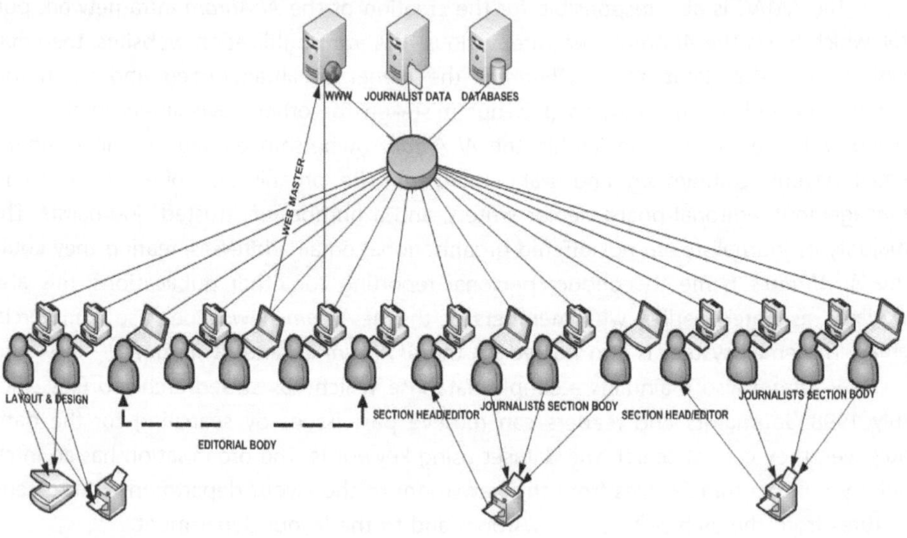

FIGURE 4
Al Dostor networking system

ICT Infrastructure at Al Dostor

Al Dostor occupies one floor in a residential building. The different sections of the newsroom are scattered across offices on the floor (see Figure 3). Internet infrastructure in the *Al Dostor* newsroom was set up a few months before the government closed the newspaper in 1998. The internet service was reintroduced with the re-establishment of the newspaper in 2005. The organisation depends on a local internet service provider for its internet service. Although the newspaper is privately owned, its history as a former government company makes its employees believe that the constant outages in internet service are planned and deliberate. As Ibrahim Mansour, the Deputy Editor of *Al Dostor*, explained:

> Whenever we complain, the companies always put the blame on the telephone company, not them, as the service providers. We are seriously thinking [about] having employees stationed at the telephone company and the internet service providers to make sure the service is running. (personal communication, 2008)

The organisation provides internet service to all staff members through a 10 MB service (see Figure 4). *Al Dostor* staff and journalists can access the internet via the internal wiring network, as well as via a wireless router. Each of the *Al Dostor* newsroom sections has between two and four computers assigned to it. Every journalist can log on to any workstation by providing a username and password to upload their stories.

Al Dostor's financial problems do not allow the organisation to upgrade its computer system. However, all available computers observed for the present study (except in two newsroom sections) were Dell Inspiration computers with an Intel Pentium IV processor, a 320 GB hard disk, and 2 GB of RAM, which are considered old models of technology to handle journalism and multimedia processing. All the computers have access to printers, fax machines, and the news organisation scanner. The organisation installed 17-inch monitors for better viewing and handling of the multimedia operation.

The computers in the layout room are Apple Macintosh for design and desktop publishing purposes. The Online Editor (webmaster) uses a technically advanced (at the time of the study) Hewlett Packard laptop with a dual-core processor, a 320 GB hard disk, and 4 GB of RAM, which makes it easier for the webmaster to work and monitor the website and feedback interactivity mechanism anytime and anywhere. The webmaster is also provided with mobile internet access for use in emergencies. The rest of the staff, however, are not provided with mobile phones. The organisation has six mobile phone lines which are paid for by the organisation for work purposes, in addition to four other lines for the editor-in-chief and other senior editors. Members of the *Al Dostor* organisation who subscribe to the Egyptian Journalism Syndicate are encouraged to take advantage of the syndicates' offers when it comes to technology. Journalists who are interested in purchasing laptops or mobile equipment can apply for an interest-free partial loan from the organisation.

Financial pressure prevents the organisation from investing in a complex intranetwork system (see Figure 4). The internal system consists of the login system and the journalists' profiles, as well as a common hard disk space for journalists and editors to share story files, pictures, and page layouts. The organisation has a complex database archive for its online news and previous issues, which is available to journalists and readers. Because of limited news resources, the organisation created "Internet Teams" whose jobs were to create an internally implemented database archive of several topics that are of interest to the organisation, i.e. alternative and opposition political systems.

The organisation's website registration and hosting are outsourced to the United States, out of the Egyptian government's reach. This is a personal initiative shouldered by *Al Dostor*'s former Editor-in-Chief, Ibrahim Eissa, because the news organisation does not have enough funds. In other terms, the website's registration is basic; it does not provide an organisation database or email service. Journalists and editors use commercial Web-based email providers, such as Yahoo, Hotmail, and Gmail. From observations

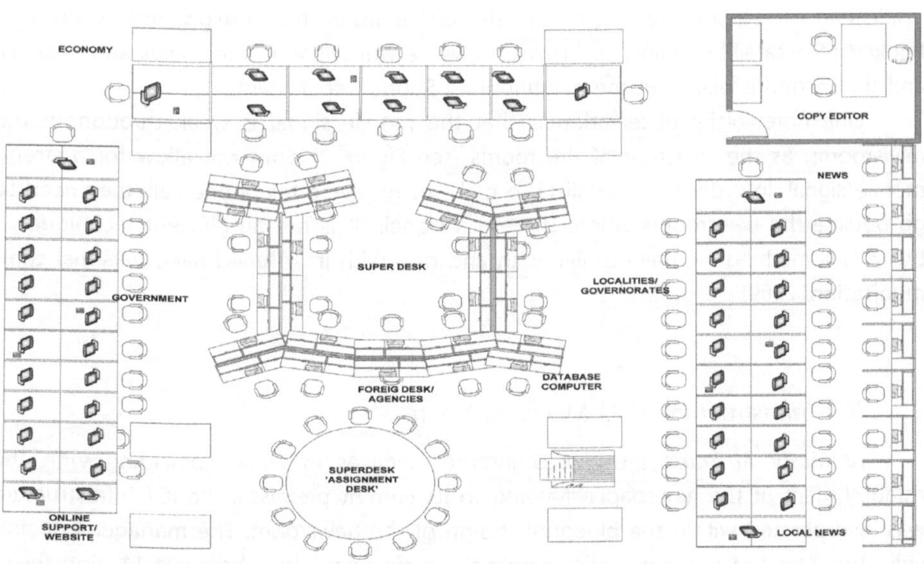

FIGURE 5
Al Masry Al Youm ICT map

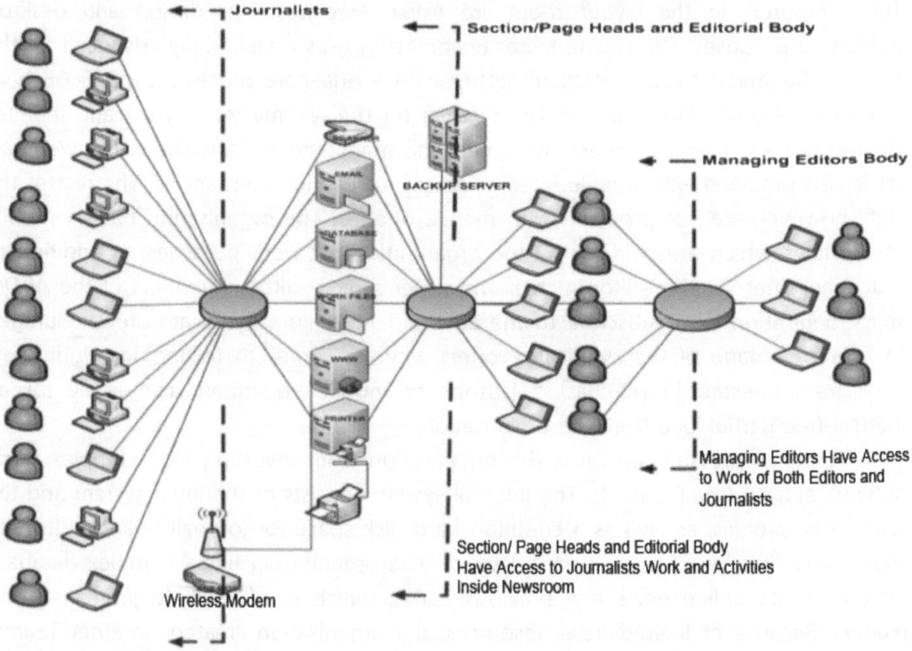

FIGURE 6
Al Masry Al Youm networking system

it was noticed that editors preferred Gmail, which they described as less prone to spam than other commercial emails.

Two telephone lines are placed in each section of the newsroom—on the desks of the newsroom editor, the deputy editor, or/senior journalist of the section/department. Mobile calls are available directly. Finally, there are two television sets available inside two newsrooms (see Figure 3)—the first is inside the Foreign Desk where it is hooked to a satellite, mainly to browse news network channels for news and analysis, and the second is placed in the neighbouring Sports Department.

One noteworthy observation is that the mobile signal is weak throughout the newsrooms, as the structure of the rooms (see Figure 3) does not allow for a strong mobile signal. In order for journalists to make or receive a telephone call, they need to go outside the newsrooms where there is a signal: "It is not an efficient technique ... but it is something we have to live with and deal with it" (Ahmed Bakr, personal communication, 2009).

ICT Infrastructure at Al Masry Al Youm

Al Masry Al Youm introduced internet services in 2004, coinciding with the establishment of the newspaper. Moving to its current premises, the ICT infrastructure was incorporated within the blueprint design of the newsroom. The management provides two forms of internet service within the newsroom. First, there is a T1 high-speed internet service for wired service, intra-network connections, and website maintenance, and second, there is a 10 MB wireless Local Area Network (LAN). All journalists have a cubicle workspace. The mobile furniture system allows for easy changes in the newsroom and each cubicle has a workstation and/or laptop access.

At the time of the first observations, the computers were new Pentium dual-core stations with flat LCD 17-inch monitors. Since 2007, all journalists who pass one of several organisation computer-training courses have received their own Dell dual-core processor laptop with mobile internet access. The training course is designed and run by the BBC Arabic service and intended for all *Al Masry Al Youm* employees, including editors. It is worth noting that in 2011, the desktop computer systems were upgraded to Dell Core 3, with 500 GB of hard disk space and 8 MB of RAM for faster internet surfing.

Management is committed to preparing their staff to be "digital journalists", able to report, type, and publish their news from the scene. In August 2008, the newspaper initiated and implemented an on-going training course designed by the BBC Arabic service in audio-visual reporting, which trains journalists to shoot and record events using handheld mobile devices. Journalists who complete the training course are offered smartphones with internet access and multimedia capabilities. All computers within the newsroom have access to a printer, a fax machine, and a scanner (see Figure 5).

Al Masry Al Youm possesses a more advanced and more secure intra-network system than both *Al Ahram* and *Al Dostor* (see Figure 6). Journalists can access their profile accounts, work email, website, and database to submit their stories, as well as track their submissions and personal story history via the intra-network system. Section/department editors have access to all of their department's journalistic work. Editors can edit their stories online, choose the running stories, archive work, and place it in the layout order. Accessing profiles is important for assessing journalists' work and development. Copy editors and senior editors have access to the entire system, including the layout and design, past and pending stories, financial information, and the human resources system. The organisation hired a specialised computer company that "Arabised" the intra-network program of the newspaper *The Guardian*. The organisation further obtained a strong database system, subscribing to different specialised media companies. Part of the multimedia department's role is to enrich the organisation's database with news from Egypt.

Twenty telephone landlines were counted inside the newsroom. The open-plan newsroom allowed easy access to all telephone lines, fax, and printing facilities. Mobile calls are also directly available. Finally, there are two Sharp 40-inch flat LCD televisions placed on two walls that can be viewed by the entire newsroom. The screens are hooked to a satellite system. During the period of study, both televisions were on 24/7, with one tuned to the Egyptian state Nile News channel and the other tuned to the pan-Arab Al Arabia channel.

The following section discusses the operationalisation of ICTs in daily news production inside the newsrooms under study.

ICTs and Daily Newsroom Routines

What makes a newsroom's identity is its influence on how news is defined, and how journalists report their news and stories. The use of technology inside newsrooms goes beyond the linear notion that "news journalism" is a "result of" technological developments. Considering the newsroom's social, cultural, and economic contextual factors is important as they influence the extent to which journalists use new technologies (Deuze 2008).

Although the *Al Ahram* journalists/editors (approximately 800 journalists) outnumber those at *Al Dostor* (approximately 100 journalists) and *Al Masry Al Youm* (approximately 200 journalists) combined, the *Al Ahram* newsroom was empty except for a few journalists throughout production hours during all tiers of observations (between 9:00 and 17:30). A total of 43 journalists/editors were present in the newsroom in 2008. These followed the story of the burning of the Egyptian Parliament. However, only 27 journalists were involved throughout the observation process. One of the main reasons for this, as interviews revealed, was that journalists do not need to be physically present in the newsroom because "it is often the case that they call their sources, write the story and dictate it by phone to the editorial secretary", as one reporter put it. Journalists often present in the newsroom were looking to break into publishing; they were also interested in using ICTs in their work.

Observations revealed that the acquisition of technology does not translate into physical availability of technology. Several journalists stated that *Al Ahram* does not have enough ICTs available for them to use. In fact, "Computers are usually out of service." This was further reflected in some of the comments provided by journalists stating that not everyone has access to the internet technologies or computers; others stated *Al Ahram* management are using obsolete technologies that cannot meet the pace of newsgathering.

Over 17 years after the introduction of internet access inside the *Al Ahram* newsroom, journalists are still struggling to embed ICTs in their daily routine. The majority of journalists do not use ICTs inside the newsroom. The quantitative survey showed that only 23.2 per cent of journalists/editors use at least one form of ICT once per day. On the other hand, 26.3 per cent of editors and senior journalists stated that they do not use ICTs inside the newsroom and do not intend to.

During the period of study, the total number of journalists using computers was limited to 14 over the span of 10 hours. Typing was seen as the primary use of computers inside the newsroom. Throughout the period of study, only six journalists brought their own laptops to work; three of these brought their own mobile dongle for a personal internet connection. The rest relied on two cables for internet connectivity.

Journalists see ICTs as a tool for their "personal use" or to "pass time at work", not as tools that can help develop their work. Examining *Al Ahram* journalists' response from the 2011 survey (see Table 1),[4] reading publications online and checking personal emails are journalists' top priorities in using the internet. Engaging with the audience, browsing the internet to search for information, and exploring multimedia materials, among other computer-assisted reporting techniques, are still rarely explored by *Al Ahram* journalists.

To complete their work, journalists depended mainly on the traditional tools, including telephones, fax, and the wire service (Salama 2009). The "traditional brown-dashed papers", which are still seen as the primary form of news and press releases from the Cabinet and other government bodies, were seen lying throughout the newsroom. Results from the survey confirm that journalists still depend on traditional forms of data gathering, such as press releases, faxes, and *Al Ahram* sources. The newest form

TABLE 1
Use of ICTs inside the Egyptian newsrooms

	Ahram					*Al Dostor*					*Al Masry Al Youm*				
	Daily	**Twice per week**	**Twice per month**	**Rarely**	**Never**	**Daily**	**Twice per week**	**Twice per month**	**Rarely**	**Never**	**Daily**	**Twice per week**	**Twice per month**	**Rarely**	**Never**
Use of ICTs inside newsrooms															
Read online publications	62.9	15.4	7.7	0	7.7	100	0	0	0	0	85.7	14.3	0	0	0
Read email	84.6	15.4	0	0	0	92.3	0	7.7	0	0	100	0	0	0	0
Participate in chat groups	0	16.7	8.3	16.7	58.3	23.1	15.4	15.4	15.4	30.8	28.6	28.6	14.5	28.6	0
Browse WWW for ideas	14.3	28.6	21.4	21.4	14.3	76.9	7.7	7.7	15.4	0	38.5	53.8	7.5	0	0
Download multimedia	23.1	30.8	0	46.2	0	61.5	15.4	15.4	15.4	0	21.4	7.1	50	21.4	0
Looking for experts	23.1	0	15.4	53.8	7.7	69.2	23.1	7.7	0	0	28.6	28.6	14.3	21.4	7.1
Journalists' sources															
Press release	50	28.6	0	0	21.4	36.4	18.2	0	9.1	36.4	14.3	14.3	28.6	14.3	28.6
Organisation source	46.2	7.7	0	23.1	23.1	25	33.3	16.7	0	24	21.4	35.7	14.3	21.4	7.1
Telephone	53.8	0	0	15.4	30.8	16.7	16.7	0	16.7	50	14.3	14.3	14.3	21.4	35.7
Fax	61.6	7.7	0	7.7	23.1	54.5	18.3	0	0	27.3	28.6	21.4	28.6	21.4	0
Satellite TV	100	0	0	0	0	53.8	23.1	7.7	0	15.4	71.4	21.4	7.1	0	0
Wire service	66.7	13.3	0	0	20	20	30.8	7.7	15.4	23.1	23.1	21.4	35.7	21.4	0
WWW	73.3	13.3	0	0	13.3	58.3	33.3	8.3	0	0	71.2	28.6	0	0	0
Email	42.9	14.4	7.1	0	35.7	46.2	15.4	0	30.8	7.7	28.9	35.7	28.6	7.7	0
ListServ	15.4	0	15.4	15.4	53.8	25	8.3	16.7	8.3	41.7	7.1	14.3	14.3	21.4	42.9
Audience feedback	0	0	0	7.7	92.3	38.5	30.8	7.7	0	23.1	14.3	7.1	21.4	42.9	14.3
Total (*N*)	37	37	37	37	37	21	21	21	21	21	27	27	27	27	27

of technology used by journalists is satellite television, with 66.7 per cent of *Al Ahram* journalists using satellite channels as a source on a daily basis. Observation showed that journalists from *Al Ahram*, especially after the revolution, were mainly logged on to Arab online television channels (mainly Al Arabia and Al Jazeera), where they searched for information on Arab affairs in the new era or "information that attacks Egypt's political stance so that it can be dealt with 'officially'" (Ahmed Metwali, personal communication, 2011).

Using new technologies is seen as a complement to traditional media (Parks 2005). In the case of *Al Ahram*, journalists cannot present their news if the internet or any of its sources are their primary source of information as management would immediately refuse to publish it. Observation showed that *Al Ahram* maintains its closed "official" chain network structure online. The management of *Al Ahram* allows for a limited number of pre-defined online activities. Furthermore, only a few journalists have access to the online content, with the management maintaining "centralised" control over the medium. The management sees the internet as an add-on to traditional news values, seeing ICT resources as untrustworthy in comparison to the traditional government "news releases".

Deuze (2009) states that developing a career in journalism in today's competitive independent and opposition media market takes more than just basic journalism writing and editing skills. The effective use of ICTs in developing stories and interacting with readers is the key to survival. This reflects the *Al Dostor* newsroom's attitude towards ICTs. Although *Al Dostor* management faces financial difficulties, making the best of the technology is the key to understanding news operationalisation inside the *Al Dostor* newsroom (Khaled El Sergany, personal communication, 2008; Mohamed Attia, personal communication, 2009). On a general note, one needs to look at *Al Dostor*'s ICT facilities as fixed items, with journalists taking turns with the technologies as teams produce their work. During the period of study, the Foreign Desk, for example, had three teams rotating to use computer stations over the course of eight hours. They took their turns with the computers to carry out three main tasks—the daily newspaper production, the weekly production, and uploads to the database. This explains why newsrooms are always busy with journalists/editors working around the clock.

During the course of study, 57 out of 65 journalists (88 per cent) were in different sections of the newsrooms using computers at some point in time. The total number of journalists using computers and the internet during the period of study was equivalent to the total number of observation hours. Journalists understood that they needed to use the technology to come up with new ideas and stories.

Reading publications online is one of the *Al Dostor* journalists' main daily activities (see Table 1). In order to overcome the government's tight control over resources, reading publications online has become a primary tool in gathering information about Egypt. *Al Dostor* is interested in hiring fresh graduates with language capabilities. During observations, three new trainee journalists were hired because they had Spanish, Italian, and German language capabilities. They were asked to browse the internet in search of news and information of interest to *Al Dostor* readers. Localising the stories sourced from the internet was a key priority in the newsroom. The majority of *Al Dostor* journalists participate in newsroom discussions and browse social media and multimedia websites searching for story ideas and interviews.

Al Dostor journalists use whatever source of information they can find in order to report their stories, especially after migrating to the Web (see Table 1). This is mainly because the news organisation tends to depend mostly on fresh graduates who have limited work experience. Information sources include copies of newspapers, magazines, press releases, and faxes mixed with printouts of emails, websites, and wire services. In order to curb government control and to receive government documents and faxes, *Al Dostor* journalists usually "have their sources inside different government ministries for tips and information" (Mansour, personal communication, 2008).

Results from the survey confirm the previous statement; the majority of journalists use the internet as their primary source of information. As for press releases, 36.4 per cent of journalists stated they use press releases on a daily basis and another 36.4 per cent stated that they never use press releases in their news coverage (see Table 1).

The *Al Masry Al Youm* newsroom centres on the utilisation of ICTs. As discussed earlier, each journalist has his or her own workstation or laptop. During the period of study, the use of computers outnumbered all other forms of technology inside the newsroom. Journalists use their computers to search the database, create and arrange their interviews, as well as type and submit articles through the organisation's internal network.

The majority of journalists use ICTs (online publications, email, chat groups, web browsing, multimedia, and searching for experts) inside the newsroom. The quantitative survey showed that 93.2 per cent of journalists/editors use at least one form of ICT at least once a day. Reading online publications and participating in chatroom discussions, especially audience feedback, is a daily ritual for journalists as these are considered sources of news and story ideas (see Table 1). *Al Masry Al Youm* journalists depend on both traditional and new media for story ideas on a daily basis, with an advantage edge for new technologies (see Table 1).

During the period of study, nearly all journalists/editors used computers at one time, with 123 out of 128 journalists (96 per cent) observed using a computer. The majority of journalists used the internet, specialised databases, document software, and email. Journalists used computers in their work production during all hours of observation inside the newsroom.

The organisation created different teams headed by an editor of the department or the vice editor. The teams work in four shifts a day, and their aim is to trace information for the newspaper production, build their own database, and train journalists on the *Al Masry* online news portal launched in 2009 and on multi-platform production (mobile publishing started in early 2010).

Conclusion: News Organisations and ICT Use Inside Newsrooms

The reinvention of newspapers in the digital age requires a change of attitude towards technology by newsrooms. The quality of newspaper leadership is directly related to its ability to innovate and manage ICTs (McLellan 2007). For *Al Ahram*, the presence of ICTs is important for the "status" of the organisation; however, *Al Ahram* management does not attach importance to the role of ICTs in developing the news content. The majority of journalists stated that the editorial team does not consider ICT applications as important as traditional newsgathering methods. Furthermore, several journalists testified that *Al Ahram* management does not encourage journalists to use new technologies. Several editors interviewed saw a faster printer as being of more value than investment in ICT infrastructure.

The organisation separates "online journalism" and "online production" from the "real newsroom". Physically, AMAC is located in a separate building next to the *Al Ahram* main building. Further, the selection and production of the online version of *Al Ahram* are done in offices inside the main *Al Ahram* building but outside the newsroom, on the seventh and tenth floors. The online teams are seen as the geeky technical guys whose job does not exceed that of making workstations start, or looking for paper jams in the photocopy machine. Their "journalism" work does not exceed archiving and providing factual information.

For *Al Ahram*'s management, the skills journalists need to possess and master relate to writing properly "in *Al Ahram* style" and keeping their "phone book up to date with the proper sources". Multimedia news production is not a priority for *Al Ahram* news management.

Al Ahram journalists were split in their attitude towards the use of ICTs. One group, the majority, followed managements' orders: "We want to keep our job and we want to build a career here" was a typical statement by a number of journalists. For another minority group, using the technology was important to develop their identity as professionals.

For *Al Dostor* news management, the presence of ICTs is important for "surviving" the daily work. Also it is important to fulfil their work as watchdogs over the regime's activities. However, although the majority of journalists believed that their organisation recognised the importance of ICTs in the newsroom, they also believed that it does not invest enough in ICTs. They complained that management did not provide enough infrastructure or updates to the current technology for a better work environment.

For management, the use of the available technology is important. Acknowledging that the limited finances are a barrier hindering the full adoption of ICTs, they still believed that "good journalism should make use of available resources and the ones we have are enough to do the daily job" (Mansour, 2011, personal communication). Further, although each newsroom represents a section in the news production, journalists were encouraged to be decentralised—that is, move outside their own sections—in searching for available workstations and resources to do their work.

Integrating ICTs into daily production and updating the website was also seen as crucial for attracting new audiences and remaining competitive in the market. Further, *Al Dostor* management also saw the importance of integrating ICTs and elements of multimedia in journalists' work. Creating a multi-skilled newsroom is one of the organisation's top priorities; however, journalists need to invest in this area themselves as well as collaborate amongst themselves in the learning process.

Although the online production teams are not fully integrated within different newsrooms as part of editorial teams, their work connects with all departments and part of their job is to assist journalists and staff in their learning process. The Multimedia Editor and multimedia staff are invited to daily meetings and are part of the overall organisation's production team, which reflects the organisation's awareness of the importance of ICTs in its operations.

Finally, for *Al Masry Al Youm*, being the most read newspaper in the Egyptian market is the primary aim behind the adoption and appropriation of new technologies.

Building the "newsroom of the future that utilises the latest of technologies is one of our goals" (Ihab El Zalaky, personal communication, 2008). *Al Masry Al Youm*'s management understands that new media technologies associated with the internet and mobile phones have become popular as people's communication tools: "We want to create our own version of modern journalism and establishing the right setting is important so journalists can create relevant news" (Nagy Mohamed, personal communication, 2011). *Al Masry Al Youm* staff are educated to understand the values of ICTs so they can effectively use the technologies. Courses designed by *The Guardian* and BBC Arabic are tailored to the needs of journalists. A development plan is under way to fully convert the organisation within five years to a multi-platform production centre.

Al Masry Al Youm realises the importance of integrating its online journalism staff with the rest of the team in its open-plan newsroom so that journalists learn from each other. As one reporter explained: "Several story ideas are created from such interaction and in the future the online content will lead the organisation news's production" (Emad Aly, personal communication, 2011 (interview)). A multi-skilled newsroom is thus at the heart of the organisation's plan and editors and journalists are under pressure to learn and embrace ICTs in their day-to-day newsmaking routines. "We thought first that if we introduce the technology journalists will [naturally] learn, but we were wrong ... one needs to understand and learn about the benefits so they can [effectively] use the technology ... only then can production and efficiency occur" (Nagwa Abdallah, personal communication, 2011).

Studying the adoption and use of ICTs inside Egyptian newsrooms has revealed wide variations between the types of organisations and their use of ICTs. As the study has revealed, the pro-government *Al Ahram* has not yet fully embraced the use of ICTs, its online presence and activities are still broadly seen as an add-on to traditional media and operations. The online version was mainly intended to expand the organisation's geographical reach in an attempt to increase popularity and therefore the circulation of its print version. Content, however, remained the same. The liberal hopes that accompanied the advent of ICTs in government media management were dashed by a strict and centralised political system, which believes that controlling content is important for dominating mass opinion and stabilising the political system. The arguments for preserving this limited freedom of expression cluster around one reason: the preservation of the nation's unity and cultural coherence.

On the other hand, independent and non-partisan newspapers are using ICTs to escape government control. For both *Al Dostor* and *Al Masry Al Youm*, journalism is about "connecting" and interacting with sources and audiences to embrace market competition. For *Al Dostor*, ICTs help journalists to become active in an increasingly dynamic and networked society. The *Al Dostor* website further serves as an open forum for debate in order to create a networked sphere where different opinions can be accessed by different stakeholders in society. Similarly for *Al Masry Al Youm*, the success of the newsroom lies in management's ability to administer a multi-skilled multimedia work centre, capable of diffusing new technologies in news creation and production. Technological convergence also helps the news organisation in diversifying news sources. In this process, *Al Masry Al Youm* management realised that print journalism and online journalism have different routines, rituals, practices, and cultures.

NOTES

1. In 2010, *Al Dostor*'s owners sold the paper to *Al Wafd* opposition party leader, in what appeared to be a government scam to control *Al Dostor* before the 2010 parliamentary elections. The new editor soon changed the editorial policy, firing the editor-in-chief and all of the editorial board. Most *Al Dostor* journalists resigned, joining the editor-in-chief in re-issuing the newspaper online. In June 2011, *Al Dostor* editor-in-chief, editorial staff, and the majority of reporters collaborated to establish the *Al Tahrir* newspaper, however keeping the *Al Dostor* online edition operating.
2. The Apple Macintosh G4 was a standard layout and design computer in many Egyptian newsrooms at the time of the study.
3. The Egyptian Journalism Syndicate is the professional body for journalists working in the press system in Egypt.
4. The table is based on the survey of the three newsrooms under study in 2011.

REFERENCES

Bruns, Axel. 2005. "Gatewatching: Collaborative Online News Production." In *Digital Formations*, edited by Steve Jones. New York: Peter Lang.

Bryman, Alan. 2004. *Social research methods*. New York: Oxford University Press.

Deuze, Mark. 2008. "Understanding journalism as a network: How it changes, and how it remains the same." *Westminster Papers in Communication and Culture* 5 (2): 4–23.

Deuze, Mark. 2009. "The people formerly known as the employers." *Journalism* 10: 315.

Domingo, David. 2006. *Inventing Online Journalism: Development of the Internet as a News Medium in Four Catalan Online Newsrooms*. Barcelona: Universitat Autonoma de Barcelona.

El Gody, Ahmed. 2012. *Journalism in a Network: the Role of ICTs in Egyptian Newsrooms* Örebro: Örebro University Press.

El Gody, Ahmed. 2014. "Online Journalism, Citizen Participation and Engagement." In *Online Journalism in Africa: Trends, Practices and Emerging Cultures*, edited by H. M. Mabweazara, O. F. Mudhai and W. Jason, 141–155. London: Routledge.

Eliasoph, Nina. 1998. *Avoiding Politics: How Americans Produce Apathy in Everyday Life*. Cambridge: Cambridge University Press.

El Gody, Ahmed. 2005. "Arab media: Did it cover the same war." In *Journalism in Global Age*, edited by Stig-Arne Nohrstedt and Rune Ottosen, 165–186. Gothenburg: Nordicom.

El Gody, Ahmed. 2007. "New Media New Censorship." In *New Media and the New Middle East*, edited by Philip Seib, 213–234. New York: Palgrave.

Grossman, G., and E. Helpman. 2005. "Outsourcing in a global economy." *Review of Economic Studies* 72: 135–159.

Hamdy Naila. 2008. "Arab Citizen Journalism Shaped by Technology: Creates a Challenge to Mainstream Media, Authorities and Media Laws." Paper prepared for Presentation at the International Association for Mass Communication Research—IAMCR, Stockholm, Sweden.

Freedom House. 2012. *Freedom on the Net 2012*. Washington, DC: Freedom House.

Information and Decision Support Centre. 2010. *Electronic Newspapers and Alternative Media*. http://www.idsc.gov.eg. last accessed 3 March 2013.

Mabweazara, Hayes M. 2011. "The Internet in the Print Newsroom: Trends, Practices and Emerging Cultures in Zimbabwe." In *News, Volume 2: Newsroom Ethnographies in the Second Decade of Internet Journalism, edited by Domingo David and Paterson, Chris,* edited by Making Online, 57–69. New York: Peter Lang.

McLellan, Michele. 2007. *News, Improved How America's Newsrooms Are Learning to Change.* Washington: CQ Press.

Ministry of Communication and Information Technology, Egypt. 2013. *Quarterly Statistics.* http://www.mcit.gov.eg/ last accessed 3 March 2013.

Murphy, Emma. 2010. "The Arab State and (Absent) Civility in New Communicative Spaces." *Third World Quarterly* 32 (5): 959–980.

Parks, Lisa. 2005. *Cultures in Orbit: Satellites and the Televisual.* Durham: Duke University Press.

Pintak, Lawrance. 2010. "Arab media and Al Jazeera Effect." In *Global Communication: Theories, Stakeholders, and Trends*, edited by Thomas McPhail, 290–304. London: Wiley-Blackwell.

Rugh, William. 1979. *The Arab Press: News Media and Political Process in the Arab World.* New York, NY: Syracuse University Press.

Rugh, William. 2004. *Arab Mass Media: Newspapers, Radio, and Television in Arab Politics.* Westport, Connecticut: Praeger.

Salama, Salama. 2009. *Al Sahafa Fauf Safeeh Sakhen [Journalism over Hot Tin Roof].* Cairo: Dar Al Ain.

Singer, Jane. 2006. "The Socially Responsible Existentialist." *Journalism Studies* 7 (1): 2–18.

Skjerdal, Terje S. 2014. "Online Journalism Under Pressure: An Ethiopian Account." In Online Journalism in Africa: Trends, Practices and Emerging Cultures, edited by M. Mabweazara Hayes, F. Mudhai Okoth, and Jason Whittaker, 89–103. London: Routledge.

Appendix A

Interviews

Abdallah, Nagwa, Senior Reporter, *Al Ahram* newspaper, 1 September 2008 and 1 September 2011.

Abdallah, Sameh, Editor, *Al Ahram Online*, 4 September 2008 and 8 July 2011.

Abdel Hasib, Mahmoud-Taymour, Managing Editor, *Al Ahram* newspaper, 6 September 2008.

Ahmed, Abdel Moati, Managing Editor, *Al Ahram* newspaper, 1 September 2008.

Ahmed, Abdel Salam, Editor, Foreign Desk, *Al Masry Al Youm* newspaper, 3 August 2008.

Aly, Emad, Reporter, *Al Masry Al Youm* newspaper, 12 August 2008.

Antar, Mohamed, Senior Reporter, *Al Masry Al Youm* newspaper, 6 August 2008.

Arafa, Eman, Reporter, *Al Dostor* newspaper, 23 September 2008.

Attia, Mohamed, Senior Reporter, *Al Dostor* newspaper, 28 September 2009.

Aziz, Moataz, Reporter, *Al Ahram* newspaper, 4 July 2012.

Badr, Ahmed, Senior Reporter, *Al Dostor* newspaper, 23 September 2008.
Bakr, Ahmed, Vice Editor, Foreign Desk, *Al Dostor* newspaper, 24 July 2009.
Eissa, Ibrahim, Editor-in-Chief, *Al Dostor* newspaper, 24 September 2008 and 20 July 2009.
Eissa, Shadi, Editor, *Al Dostor* newspaper, 28 September 2009.
El Amir, Mohamed, Editor, Foreign Desk, *Al Dostor* newspaper, 12 August 2009.
El Gallad, Magdy, Editor-in-Chief, *Al Masry Al Youm*, 6 August 2008.
El Hawary, Mohamed, Reporter, Multimedia Department, *Al Masry Al Youm* newspaper, 6 August 2008.
El Sergany, Khaled, Senior Editor, *Al Dostor* newspaper, 5 September 2008.
El Tohaiby, Adel, Editor, *Al Ahram* Management and Computer Center, 20 July 2009.
El Zalaky, Ihab, Multimedia Editor, *Al Masry Al Youm* newspaper, 2 August 2008 and 18 August 2008.
Emad, Zakareya, Reporter, *Al Ahram* newspaper, 3 September 2008.
Essmat, Nourhan, Reporter, *Al Masry Al Youm* newspaper, 3 July 2009.
Korashi, Essam, Senior Managing Editor, *Al Ahram* newspaper and Editor-in-Chief, *Al Ahram Weekly*, 1 September 2009.
Mahamoud, Ahmed, Senior Editor, *Al Masry Al Youm* newspaper, 6 September 2008.
Mansour, Ibrahim, Managing Editor, *Al Dostor* newspaper, 9 August 2008 and 20 August 2011.
Metwali, Ahmed, Reporter, *Al Ahram* newspaper and Editor, *Al Ahram Online*, 3 September 2009 and 13 August 2011.
Metwali, Sami, Managing Editor, *Al Ahram* newspaper, 24 August 2008.
Mohamed, Hazem, Reporter, Foreign Desk, *Al Dostor* newspaper, 12 August 2011.
Mohamed, Nagy, Editor, *Al Masry Al Youm* newspaper, 11 August 2009.
Nassar, Gallal, Editor, *Al Ahram* newspaper, 4 September 2009.
Nasser, Nessrin, Reporter, *Al Masry Al Youm* newspaper, 15 August 2008.
Salem, Ahmed, Reporter, *Al Ahram* newspaper, 20 September 2009 and 3 July 2012.

JOURNALISTS' TWITTER NETWORKS, PUBLIC DEBATES AND RELATIONSHIPS IN SOUTH AFRICA

Peter Verweij and **Elvira van Noort**

Journalists at major media houses in South Africa use Twitter as a journalistic tool for crowd sourcing, breaking news events, live blogging and to balance, check and cultivate sources. This paper analyses the use of the social network platform by the top 500 South African journalists. The findings suggest that pluralism and openness are important characteristics of the South African Twitter network. Although two strong sub-networks can be detected, we conclude that they give structure to the network and enhance the role of journalists in public debates and democratic decision-making. This is shown in the analysis of three trending news topics related to politics and crime. The last trending topic of the study questions the process of the individualization of journalism through Twitter. The paper concludes by confronting its generic findings from the perspectives and opinions of leading journalists and editors.

Journalism and Social Networks

The "network paradigm" relates to fundamental characteristics of modern society (Castells 2000). This paradigm does not only refer to physical structures, the worldwide digital connections associated with the internet, but also to our social relationships and our myriad ways of communicating. Our social relationships are transforming from face-to-face relations to a broader-based network of contacts wherein basic constraints like time and space are no longer important. After the mass introduction of computers and computer networks in the 1990s, e-mail appeared as an easy way to communicate. In contemporary times, social media have been added to our communication mix: with Twitter considered a "newsy" tool, Facebook predominantly used for social events and LinkedIn for professional contacts. These platforms share the same characteristic as they are forms of social network-based communication (Huberman et al. 2009). Huberman revealed that there are few actual interactions between people on Twitter except for those few that matter and reciprocate their attention.

The analysis of social networks was deeply influenced by these developments. First, because our social relationships became more and more network based. And second, the technology or the toolbox to conduct a social network analysis was further developed. From more academic tools like UCINET and Pajek to easy-to-use tools like NodeXL (Hansen, Shneiderman, and Smith 2011), which is an add-on for Microsoft Excel, and open source-based Gephi (Hirst 2011). The initial centrality measures used in analysis were refined and listed (Wasserman and Faust 1994). With these developments, it is safe to say that these tools can now be effectively handled by journalists to produce data-driven stories (Meyer 2004; Verweij 2012a).

Network-based communication through social media transformed the classical model of mass communication. Society moved from a sender–receiver model with a two-step flow (Baran 2011) to *We the Media* (Gillmor 2004). The differences between these two models can be summarized in the following keywords: one-way versus two-way (interactive); top-down versus bottom-up; closed versus open; institutional journalism versus individualized journalism; former public versus we media; atomized public versus community building and individual versus crowd sourcing (Rosen 2012).

Twitter is a fitting illustration of these characteristics of change in communication. The tool includes all "we-media" aspects. New media in general (from online newspapers and blogs to social media) transform the process of communication by making it more open, pluralistic and democratic because it gives more room to engage in public debates. In addition, the changes in the way we communicate have consequences for the media, in general, and for journalism, in particular (Bardoel and Deuze 2001).

There are three interesting trends in academic research: the position of the journalist, the changes in journalism practice and the role of the public. First, in the transition from old to new media the position of the journalist becomes more individualized (Bardoel 2010), whereas previously their position was strongly based on the position of the medium he or she worked for. The media houses and titles are not the only brands, individual journalists are becoming more and more brands in themselves.

Second, there are the changes in journalism practice. A topic that has been the subject of wide research is how media, journalists in general, use Twitter (Pew Foundation 2011). One aspect in these growing researches is the role Twitter plays in the journalistic process of newsgathering (Cohen 2009; Farhi 2009). Twitter is a source for news, which is miles away from the classical approach (Hermida 2009; Gans 1980). Hermida's ideas about Twitter as an "alarm bell", and crowd sourcing, open up a new era for journalism (Verweij 2010). In addition, Twitter is not only a source but also a medium. Media use it to enhance their digital news first strategy to broadcast the latest news and headlines on Twitter.

Finally, there is the interactivity of the medium, which opens up new ways for starting, engaging and deepening the public debate. A first attempt to bring together Twitter, public debate and social network analysis was an analysis of connections between political reporters and members of the Parliament in The Netherlands (Verweij 2012b). It was interesting to notice that the connections between members of parliament and reporters were not exclusively ordered along the traditional ideological and religious lines. The idea of a political communication elite (Luyendijk 2010) could not be confirmed, but instead the study showed a multi-centered network of different groups of journalists. An open, non-elite structure of the political reporters' network is a condition for democracy and public debate. This research builds on this earlier work while focusing on the South African context.

South Africa, Journalism and Social Networks

Theories and research findings discussed above mostly originate from studies based on journalism and reporting in the Western world. Transferring them without reflection to another context, especially Africa, is not without problems. However, post-independence South Africa shares a number of characteristics with Western countries: such as their organization of the media and standards for journalism practice. Nonetheless, the involvement of the public in debates is different because of the social deprivation of the bulk of its citizens, a challenge directly connected to South Africa's apartheid past.

The permeation of digital technologies into various social structures in Africa has given rise to discussions around the so-called "digital divide". However, in the specific case of South Africa, the gap is smaller than in other African countries. Second, the internet revolution, or the creation of a network society, is facilitated and bridged by the wide distribution of cell phone networks across Africa.[1] Thus, the digital revolution in (South) Africa is a mobile revolution. LAN-based connections to the internet were a prerogative of universities, governmental institutions and companies while mobile internet and WiFi conquered the rest of the population. Nowadays visiting websites, news portals, sending e-mail and using social media like Twitter and Facebook is shaping a new routine for South African professionals such as journalists. This is reflected in an interesting moderated list of over 500 journalists on Twitter.[2]

Besides professionals, the public is also active on the internet and in particular Twitter; 5.33 million South Africans are using Facebook on the Web and 2.43 million were on Twitter by the end of August 2012 (WorldWideWorx 2012). When compared to South Africa's general population of 51,770,560 (Stats SA 2011), just under 5 percent of South Africans are tweeting. This number might seem relatively small but according to the South African Social Media Landscape 2012 study, Twitter shows a growth rate of around 100,000 new users a month—which is equal to Facebook (WorldWideWorx 2012). Together these users sent 9.6 million tweets on average on Mondays and again on Fridays (WorldWideWorx 2012), while the rest of the week is slightly below that figure.

The role of journalism in public debates is influenced by the political context in South Africa. This context has the following characteristics (Harber and Renn 2010). The African National Congress (ANC) became the leading political party after apartheid. After 10 years in government it became clear that the political promises that were made were not realized. In other words, the socio-economic situation of the majority of people has not fundamentally changed. The situation has only changed for a small part of the black population. But at the same time the government on all levels struggled to spend money according to the budget, which raised discussions of fraud, nepotism and the misuse of power. Corruption, fraud, crime, the misuse of public money and mismanagement became trending topics in politics and the media is eager to expose the wrongdoers (Harber and Renn 2010).

Confronted with this situation and the critical and leading role of journalism, the government proposed a bill for regulation of the press that was passed by Parliament in April 2013. All the negative PR sits uneasily with the government which is expected to pass the "Protection of State Information Bill" in June 2013. This Bill aims to protect state secrets against whistle blowers and investigative journalists. Just under 400 civil society organizations have joined in the Right2Know campaign to protest against the Bill. The South African National Editors' Forum (SANEF) argues it makes investigative journalism more difficult and may silence potential whistle blowers in corruption cases as it criminalizes knowingly accessing classified information that could be potentially in the public interest. This Information Bill could have a chilling effect on public debates by the media, including the activities on social media platforms such as Twitter.

Research Design

The emergence of a network society in South Africa, indicated by the use of Twitter by the public and journalists, in the context of the political problems of a one-party democracy, makes it interesting to apply social network analysis to the use of Twitter by journalists in South Africa. Such an analysis could give an impression of the openness, transparency and pluralism of the public debates and the role of journalists. Twitter is, of course, not identical with that debate but can give an indication of the involvement of journalists. The leading question of this research is: What is the structure of the Twitter network among journalists in South Africa and how does this network contribute to public debate?

There are various important aspects that need to be studied. First there is the Twitter network between the journalists. What is the structure of this network? Is it open or closed? Is there a leading elite or are there different centres or groups? From the perspective of democratic decision-making, it would be important to have a pluralistic network. If the network is closed and in the hands of an elite, the public debate could completely be controlled by that elite. And that would have a chilling effect on public debate. Therefore, we start with the analysis of the structure of the Twitter network of South African journalists. Out of the 500 selected journalists on Twitter, we reconstructed the social network. We used two tools for analysis: Gephi and NodeXL. Both resulted in the same network graph and centrality measures such as In-Degree and Page rank. Especially In-Degree is interesting, because it lists the number of followers of a journalist on Twitter and could therefore be interpreted as being an important news source. A higher In-Degree could therefore be interpreted as a higher ranking on authority in the network.

Details of the structure of the network can be found by paying attention to the medium- print or audio-visual the journalists are working for. Finally, we pay attention to different sub-groups in the network using an algorithm (developed by Wakita and Tsurumi 2007). This algorithm creates sub-groups by adding these individuals to a sub-network of a group under the condition that it enlarges the density. So the algorithm tries to find groups with a higher network density than the total network density. The problem of course is the interpretation, which is a general problem in network analysis. Groups are the result of a mathematical calculation and that figure representing a group needs to get a meaning in the real world.

Second, is this Twitter network different from other journalism Twitter networks? We compare the general characteristics of the South African network with British and Dutch journalism Twitter networks (*Guardian* 2011; Verweij 2012b). The dimensions for comparing the networks are limited to general network measures as density and distance of the network.

Having analyzed the journalistic Twitter network in general, we confront questions on how involved journalists are in the various public discussions. In order to analyze the role of journalists on Twitter in public debates, we selected three examples. These examples are typical for major political issues in South Africa and are related to issues like corruption, fraud or crime. Our focus on the role of journalists and the public is based on three examples: the case of the former premier of the Eastern Cape province Balindlela; the debate over the use of public money for President Zuma's new home: Nkandlagate and the Oscar Pistorius murder investigation.

This academic approach is not complete without views from journalism practice. We conducted four detailed and intensive interviews with leading journalists focusing on their views about Twitter and public debates. The conclusions form the last part of this research.

SA 500 Journalists Twitter Network

This data set of 500 South African journalists on Twitter was available from the Hacks List, a project of South African journalist Alastair Otter. Otter explains on his website that the list is largely self-moderated and that any South African journalist can sign up. All the information is pulled from public data (Twitter profiles) except for the media house they work for—that is provided by journalists themselves.[3] We downloaded their connections in August 2012 and analyzed them in two open-source programs: Gephi and NodeXL. The network consists of 506 individuals who share 2503 connections between them—this gives a density of 9 percent. This figure means that only 9 percent of all possible connections in this particular Twitter network are realized. It is a low figure, meaning that this Twitter network is not closely connected. The average distance in the network is almost two steps (1.9). Although the network is not highly connected, a majority of the members could easily be contacted in less than two steps. Meaning contacting a person is possible via another person who is in between. So journalists on Twitter in this sample can easily contact one another as they are closely following each other.

Authority

Having 506 journalists in the network, the first question is who is the most important; or who has the highest authority? There are various measures but they all come to the same result. In-Degree (number of incoming contacts; i.e. on Twitter the number of people following) gives a measure for being an interesting news source. Table 1 gives the top 20 for In-Degree. It is interesting to note that the majority of journalists in this top 20 are connected to print journalism or the online edition of a print newspapers. In their tweets they are adding information to a news event or commenting on the event. Two reporters of Radio 702 are on the list, because they use Twitter in their radio broadcasting to communicate with their listeners. There is one newspaper, the *Mail & Guardian* (M&G), a weekly, that has a leading position in this top 20. The implication is that for the M&G Twitter is an important tool and because they are very active on Twitter, their presence on this list is higher. Secondly, they are an important source of news, scoring highly on authority. The position of two journalism academics, Guy Berger and Anton Harber, is remarkable on this list. And finally, freelance journalists are also very active on Twitter and enjoy considerable authority.

TABLE 1
Top 20 for authority in the SA 500 network

Twitter profile name and In-Degree	Medium	Group
ferialhaffajee 361	*City Press*	5
nicdawes 327	*Mail & Guardian*	0
gussilber 298	Freelance	1
mandywiener 288	*EyeWitness News*	4
phillipdewet 269	*Mail & Guardian*	1
stephengrootes 268	*EyeWitness News*	4
maxdupreez 264	Freelance	4
hartleyr 262	*Sunday Times*	4
adriaanbasson 234	*City Press*	4
702johnrobbie 227	Radio 702	4
bruceps 227	*Business Day*	1
verashni 217	*Mail & Guardian*	3
mandyldewaal 217	*Daily Maverick*	0
antonharber 217	Freelance	4
carienduplessis 214	*City Press*	4
art2gee 213	Freelance	1
guyberger 211	Personal	0
shapshak 207	Stuff	1
akianastasiou 205	Radio 702	1
brankobrkic 205	*Daily Maverick*	1

On average the individuals in this top 20 have written 10,000 tweets (with a maximum of 23,000 and a minimum of 2300). Although the range is quite broad, the high average indicates that these individuals are active on Twitter; and as representatives of the journalistic profession it measures the importance of Twitter for journalists.

Figure 1 is a visualization of this top 20 list. The size of the font for name is set so the vertices (individuals) with the higher In-Degree are bigger. The impression from the number of edges (connecting lines) that this top 20 network is highly connected is correct. The density in this sub-network is 83 percent and the average distance is 1. The conclusion is that this group is an elite or clique in the bigger network of 500. These individuals listen to and follow each other on Twitter closely. They take the lead in discussions between journalists and the wider public on Twitter. However, their position should not be overestimated, they have a leading role but in respect to the "openness" on Twitter it is not the case that they control the debates. Secondly, the importance of each member of the top 20 is not equal, as reflected by the font size. Finally, it is clear that a journalist who wants to become an authority on Twitter, should at least be connected to individuals in this sub-group. Journalists could become important on Twitter by connecting to some of these high-ranking individuals.

Table 2 lists the number of tweeting journalists per media house or title. For example, the M&G has 20 tweeting journalists, which is 4 percent of the total number in our sample. The last column lists journalists with the highest authority and Nic Dawes takes the lead at the M&G. In terms of authority on this list, we notice first the importance of freelance journalists. They probably use Twitter for getting jobs, finding news or commenting on news, as well as for referring or linking a wider readership to their published stories. In second position is the M&G, a weekly which is a hard-copy newspaper as well as online. The *EyeWitness News* (EWN) is an online news organization

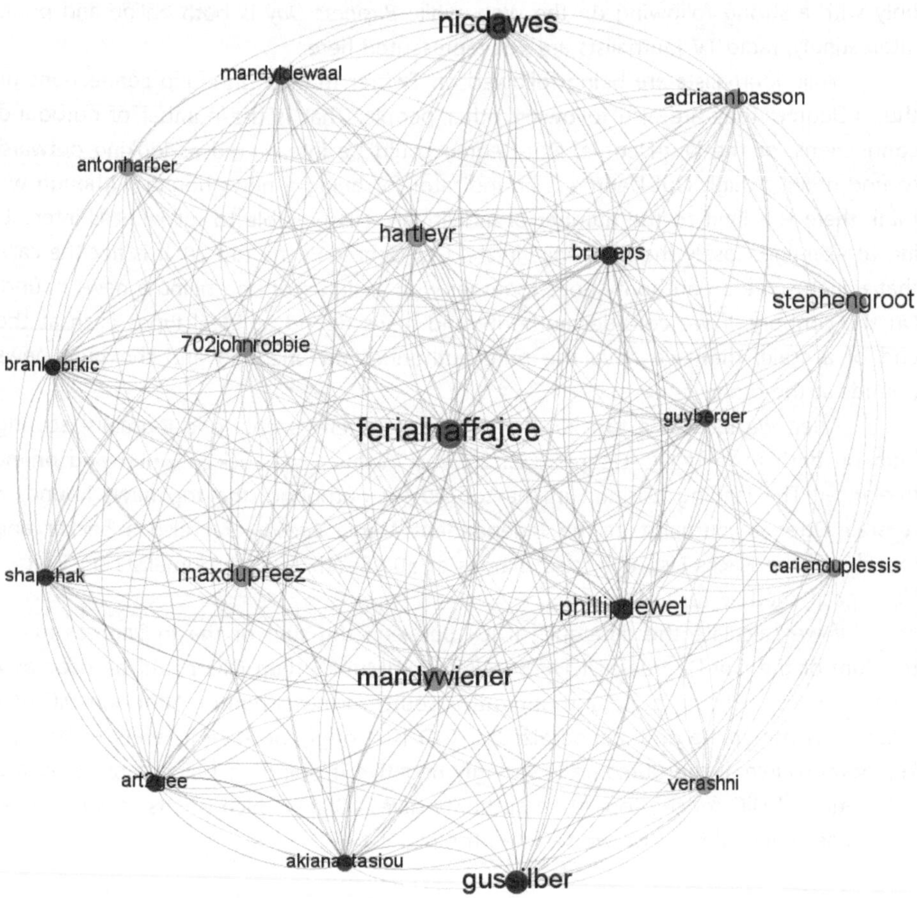

FIGURE 1
Top 20 authorities in the SA 500 network

TABLE 2
Top 10 media on Twitter

	N	%	Twitter profile name
Freelance journalists	89	18	gussilber
Mail & Guardian	20	4	nicdawes
EyeWitness News	16	3	mandywiener
Business Day	14	3	bruceps
eNews	14	3	nbikitsha
Caxton, local and community	12	2	amandzing
The Star	12	2	kevinmccallum
Daily Maverick	10	2	mandyldewaal
New Age	10	2	rylandfisher
News24	9	2	janniemom
Nuus24	9	2	mynuus24

only with a strong following on the Web, while *Business Day* is both online and print. Interestingly, radio/TV journalists are not represented here.

While journalists are being followed on Twitter through inbound connections or the In-Degree, they are also following other people. That is the number of outbound connections, or the Out-Degree. Out-Degree could be interpreted as looking outward to find news. A high Out-Degree is an indicator for being a news hound. Although we think there is a limit to the number of individuals it is possible to follow, it is interesting to examine closely the difference in the Out-Degree in the top 20. It is not the case that a high score on authority goes together with a high score on being a news hound. On the contrary, if we consider authority and news hound as ideal types each at the end of a scale, then we have the pure authorities on one end and the pure news hounds at the other.

When we look at a top 20 on Out-Degree, there is only one journalist scoring high on both In- and Out-Degree: @art2gee or Arthur Goldstuck, a writer and online freelancer. The leading position in the top 20 for outbound, the top news hound, is Alastair Otter, a journalist at the Independent Media Group, but also a hacker and founder of the Hacks List, the list of names of 500 South African journalists on Twitter. He is positioned 26 for In-Degree.

If we calculate the difference (DIO) between the sum of the In-Degrees minus the sum of the Out-Degrees: DIO = SUM(in) − SUM(out), then DIO could be used as a measurement for being more authority/news source or news hound. Although DIO as a measure is not stable and standardized, if DIO is strongly positive it refers to being a key news source; if the outcome is strongly negative it points to being a news hound. Calculation of DIO for the top 20 on authority gives +3063, which points to a key news source, as expected because we selected the highest In-Degrees.

Groups

This section directs attention to the sub-groups in the network of the 500 tweeting journalists. The construction of sub-groups in the network is based on the algorithm developed by Wakita and Tsurumi, trying to enlarge the density in each sub-group. It should be noted that the density in these groups is in general not more than twice the density in the total network (18 percent maximum). These groups are more closely related than the total network, but they are far away from the density of the top 20 authority network.

In the Twitter 500 network six groups or clusters can be constructed, as shown in Table 3. The problem is naming the groups resulting from the calculations of the algorithm. We have named them on the basis of the employer or media house of the tweeting journalists. Group 0 has 145 members, of which 28 percent of the total number in the network and DIO score refer to news hound. The group mainly consists of journalists working for newspapers. The leading "Twitterati"[4] is Nic Dawes of the M&G. M&G return again in group 3, where the @Verashni (Deputy Editor Verashni Pillay) plays a similar role as Dawes in group 0, but this group is mostly composed of journalists of Media24 and has a DIO score referring to news hound. Gussilber, a freelance journalist, is heading the sub-group of business and financial newspapers. This group is smaller, because it is more specialized and their DIO score refers slightly to being a news

TABLE 3
Groups in the Twitter network

Top Twitterati	Group	DIO score	*N* Twitterati	%	Composition
nicdawes	0	−478	145	28	News and background
gussilber	1	+90	91	18	Business/finance/ICT
edenvalejourno	2	−56	10	2	Local and community papers
verashni	3	−295	56	11	Media24 newspapers
mandywiener	4	+251	169	33	News and analysis
ferialhaffajee	5	+211	35	7	Sports

source. Sub-groups are not homogeneous, composed of journalists of one media house or newspaper. The biggest group, group 4, has 169 members and is dedicated to news and analysis. The DIO score refers to news source. It is remarkable to see that a journalist, Mandy Wiener, of the online news-only EWN, takes the lead here. This points to the fact that online media are more active on Twitter.

Mail & Guardian

So far our analysis has revealed an important and leading role for M&G. The question, however, is how are the journalists of M&G divided over the various groups? Table 4 attempts to provide an overview of this.

Table 4 shows a division over the different groups in the network. Six M&G journalists are connected to the news and opinion group where freelance journalists are in the majority. Nine of them are connected to the news and analysis group where other leading media are represented as well. The DIO score indicates news hound. Journalists at the M&G are connected to various sub-groups in the network, related to different beats and topics. This spread is important to have a variety of sources, which add to balanced reporting.

Because of the pivotal role of M&G in the 500 network it is important to analyse their network. The mutual connections within the M&G Twitter network are shown in Figure 2. The size of the profile photo corresponds with the authority within that group, with @NicDawes being the biggest. It is obvious that the number of connections in this graph is higher than the average in the network. The M&G Twitter network consists of 20 individuals. Their average distance is 1.2 and the density is 45 percent. This is another closely connected group. Remarkable is the fact that the DIO score for

TABLE 4
Number of *Mail & Guardian* journalists per group

Group	*N*
0 News and background	6
1 Business/finance/ICT	3
3 Media24 newspapers	2
4 News and analysis	9

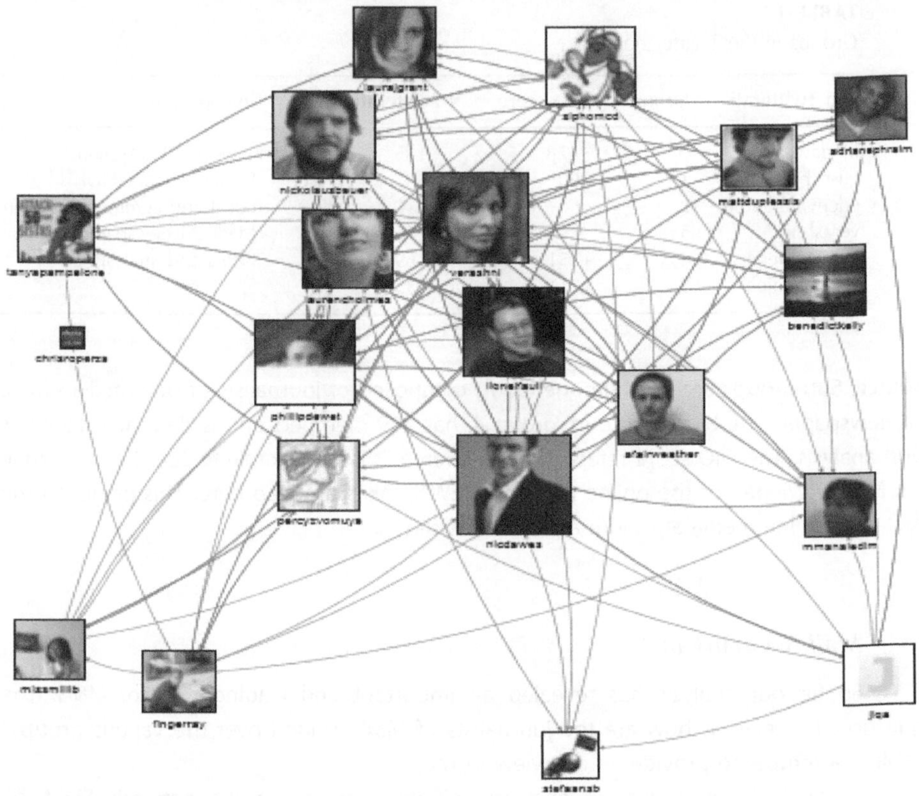

Created with NodeXL (http://nodexl.codeplex.com)

FIGURE 2
The Twitter network of M&G journalists

the M&G network is 0, meaning a balance between news source and news hound. Combined with the position they have in the top 20 on authority, this is a leading group on Twitter. They are not able to control the debate on Twitter, but are at least able to set directions and topics of the discussions.

Comparison

The general picture of the 500 South African journalists on Twitter shows that journalists follow each other in a network with a low density, but with an average distance which makes it easy to connect to another with a few steps. This was also one of the conclusions of research in the United Kingdom and The Netherlands (Verweij 2012b). In that respect the South African network does not differ fundamentally from the Western world. The reason for this is that journalists are sources of news, following each other is simply following sources and finding news. In the South African as in the European networks, sub-groups can be constructed. These sub-groups create structure in the network, but are not in the position of complete control. In general, European and South African Twitter networks have an open structure. This structure facilitates free and open discussion, providing a firm basis for democratic decision-making.

Although the general structure of the South African Twitter network is not fundamentally different from European networks, there are a few remarkable positions. First, we constructed a top 20 on authority. What is striking is the density in this group, together with the distance. The conclusion drawn from this top 20 group is that the Twitter elite is inescapable. However, one should be careful not to attribute too much power to this group. Given the openness of the Twitter network in general, it is safe to conclude that this group can set the agenda for discussion, and also influence the directions of discussion. This is an important role in South Africa's political discussion, especially given the lack of a strong political opposition rendering it a *de facto* one-party democracy. Their Twitter ratings are giving them the opportunity to voice criticism and opposition against the government.

Second, the M&G network is characterised by a high density and short distance. What makes the M&G network influential is the relations with the top 20 on authority. And on top of this, their connections with the other subgroups in the Twitter network. The position of the M&G group provides a firm basis for investigative journalism and political debate related to main problems in South African society and government. The position of M&G as one of the influential newspapers of the opposition is reflected by their Twitter ratings.

It is tempting to conclude that the M&G and its journalists are leading in the Twitter network. But one should not overlook other factors in the network that tone down M&G's top position. First, the number one spot in the Top 20 is reserved for the Editor of the *City Press* (@FerialHaffajee); and second, journalists from other media, like EWN, rank highly as well; and finally, a number of freelancers have a similarly high position. The graph of the top 20 for authority shows a more connected network of journalists from various other media. Journalists at the M&G are also closely related to other groups in the Twitter network. The South African Twitter network can therefore best be characterized as open and poly-centered, consisting mostly of newspaper journalists, but with radio and TV in second position.

One can conclude that the South African Twitter network of journalists is characterized by pluralism; notwithstanding the leading role of the top 20 on authority and the M&G sub-network. The openness and pluralism expressed by the various sub-groups in the Twitter network are important prerequisites for shaping public debate and in the end democratic decision-making.

To show the role of these groups of journalists in the Twitter network in public debates, we conducted three case studies of the role of journalists and the public focusing on Balindlela, Nkandlagate and Pistorius.

Case Studies

Balindlela

Nosimo Balindlela is the former Premier of the South African Eastern Cape province. She was a member of the ANC but lost ground in the struggle for the presidency between Zuma and Mbeki and joined the break-away party Congress of the People (COPE). In November 2012 she joined yet another party, the Democratic Alliance (DA)—South Africa's main opposition party led by Helen Zille. Balindlela's political transformations—changing parties three times—triggered a raging discussion on Twitter. Our analysis shows a network of 1350 individuals sharing 2215 connections. This is a totally unconnected network with a density close to zero, which is very typical for a discussion on Twitter. Also the average distance between the individuals is large.

Of interest is that within a couple of hours 1350 individuals took part in the heated online discussion. The most important topics in this Twitter discussion included the following issues:

- Balindlela was not a very effective Premier, especially in fighting fraud and balancing the budget.
- This attitude was enforced by her personal style: the traditional dress and walking bare feet.
- Her move to join the DA was explained as political opportunism, a political rolling stone switching alliances from ANC to COPE and finally DA.
- Is joining the DA an asset? Does this move make the DA a more acceptable party for the black population in the Eastern Cape?

If we take incoming connections on Twitter—In-Degree—as a measure, we notice that there are two leading groups in this discussion on the Twitter network: a group of individuals around the DA and its party leader Helen Zille, who are welcoming Balindlela and are defending her decision. Second, there is a group of various journalists from different media, who are questioning the decision, and are firing up the debate. The rest of the participants (although they can be split up in more detailed groups) are citizens, party members and activists, adding positive and negative comments to the debate.

The position of the following journalists on Twitter is worth paying attention to: @ewnreporter (EWN team), @stephengrootes (Stephen Grootes, host of Radio 702 and Cape Talk radio, political reporter at EWN), @mandywiener (Mandy Wiener, reporter at EWN) and @city_press (*City Press* newspaper online team). They all play a central role in the discussion. Notice that Grootes and Wiener score high on authority as news sources; and Wiener also leads group 4 about news and analysis, also with a news source character. Zille's DA party has a majority in Cape Town, where EWN has one of their head offices.

Nkandlagate

President Jacob Zuma's renovation of his rural home in Nkandla using 248 million rand of the taxpayers' money leading to accusations of misusing public funds sparked a wild outcry on many fronts including on Twitter. The case is dubbed "Nkandlagate". The Twitter network of individuals focusing on this scandal is again a snapshot, this time taken on November 24, 2012. In this discussion 841 people who share 1321 connections took part. As is expected, the average distance between the individuals is large and the density is low. Of particular importance is the role of journalists: when we look again at In-Degree we can see most of the individuals involved are journalists trying their best to get attention for their publication about this topic but also crowd sourcing through asking the public for comments to use in their stories.

Several journalists from our top 20 on authority play a leading role in this ongoing discussion; e.g. @adriaanbasson (Adriaan Basson, assistant editor at *City Press*) and @ferialhaffajee. Interestingly radio talkshows took a leading role in the Twitter discussion of this scandal; e.g. @capetalk567 (Cape Town news and talk station), @702johnrobbie (John Robbie, host of Radio 702), generally using Twitter for crowd sourcing and presenting the tweets during the programme.

From both examples it is evident that journalists on Twitter play an important role in public debates. Although journalists from our top 20 network and from the M&G network are participating, their role is limited. It is important to notice the influence of other media organizations, for example, the *City Press* and various radio programmes as noted above.

Pistorius

Oscar Pistorius became the first amputee to win an able-bodied world track medal in 2011 and in 2012 he was the first double leg amputee to participate in the Summer Olympics. In that same year he set world records in the Paralympics. The rising star was charged with the murder of his girlfriend Reeva Steenkamp after he had fatally shot her in his home on February 14, 2013.

Between February 14 and 20, 2013 the hash tag #OscarPistorius was trending worldwide on Twitter. In total 1,306,313 tweets with the hash tag #OscarPistorius were sent in seven days—that is 130 tweets per minute. The Pistorius case reveals other aspects of journalists in the Twitter network (Verweij 2013a, 2013b). It is a perfect example of the "alarm bell" concept (Hermida 2009). The Twitter alarm bell goes off when *Beeld*, an Afrikaans newspaper, tweets: "Oscar Pistorius skiet sy vriendin in sy huis dood omdat hy glo dink sy is 'n inbreker" (translated: "Oscar Pistorius fatally shoots his girlfriend in his home because he believes she is a burglar"). Journalists dive into the breaking news story. Within no time the number of tweets is up to a quarter million. There is a familiar pattern: the first tweets share the news, and later on they shift to reasoned opinions and statements as well as jokes and comments (Verweij 2010).

During the Magistrate's Court hearing about Pistorius' bail application, Twitter becomes the only direct news source because cameras and microphones are not allowed in the courtroom. But on Twitter all the information/facts need to be spread in 140-character tweets. This takes special skills for a court reporter: the ability to be concise but detailed, to be able to describe emotions and observations, to keep the facts straight and to make sure each tweet is a follow-up on the previous message so that the audience can keep track of the unfolding story. These skills were displayed by a cross-section of journalists. EWN reporter Barry Bateman played a leading role in this case. His followers on Twitter went up from 17,429 on February 15 to 122,743 on February 21. His mentions went up to 89,592.

From this one can conclude that he became an important source on Twitter, broadcasting the latest news from the court, and explaining to the public what was going on. This shows that Twitter gives individual journalists a strong platform for connecting with their various stakeholders. It further demonstrates that the quality of reporting is not related to the reputation of a media house. The journalist is the brand and he or she builds their own reputation, thus on Twitter the credibility of a medium is transferred to the individual reporter. The Twitter network therefore drives "individualization" among journalists. This implies that in public debates and discussion within society the role of the media could decrease in favour of the increasing centrality of individual journalists who have the skills to tell a story on Twitter.

Journalism Practice: Perspectives from Practitioners

To give these findings a perspective from journalism practice, we conducted interviews with four journalists selected from the top 20 leading on authority as noted earlier (see Table 1). We spoke to Ferial Haffajee of *City Press* (No. 1), freelance journalist Gus Silber (No. 3), radio journalist and host of Radio 702 Aki Anastasiou (No. 19) and his colleague Stephen Grootes (No. 6). Their opinions about Twitter reflect both the role of the news hound and news source.

Haffajee stated that Twitter "has enhanced my journalism and enriched it in many ways". She argued that she is now "faster, sharper and perhaps more interesting because of Twitter." As editor, Haffajee noted that she uses Twitter to "break news, float opinions, fine tune editorial thinking [and] take the pulse of a section of our reading public". These developments pointed to a changing news routine and the way news is assembled, including the expansion of ideas and setting of an agenda. Similarly, Silber highlighted that Twitter is unique in that in the mainstream media "you can't allow for debates like this, in which so many different groups of people are heard, for example on television." Further comparing Twitter to television and other traditional media Silber stated that "it will be a while before Twitter is seen as just another media channel. It still has a powerful air of novelty and trendiness about it". But "hardly any major news event these days goes unaccompanied by analysis, in other media, of what people are saying about it on Twitter".

For Silber, media houses need to have journalists who are capable of "filter[ing] information and spread[ing] both news and commentary that is easy to digest ... It's still a relatively new tool and journalists still struggle to switch from the traditional media mindset to publishing online". Anastasiou from Radio 702 agrees that using Twitter as a journalistic tool is a different kind of reporting. "With the Pistorius case the pace was so quick you could easily get lost in the conversation". He adds that journalists need a different set of skills as Twitter is what radio was 20 years ago. "It is where people get their breaking news and it is fascinating to see how it has changed the way we do journalism".

Some of the characteristics of Twitter are new to journalists: its immediacy, the direct connections with the public and the skill to tell a story in 140 characters. For Anastasiou this professional transformation is "like having your finger on the button of a nuclear missile, if it goes wrong it goes horribly wrong and you can't stop the missile!". His colleague at Radio 702, Grootes, similarly argued that:

> Twitter gets information out so quickly, it is much harder to control. This means that facts get into the public domain before any gatekeeper, whether an editor or otherwise can stop it. This has some risks but is generally a very positive development, information wants to be free. Twitter allows for that and keeps it cheap!

Anastasiou was the second journalist to tweet about the Pistorius incident (referred to earlier), on the day of his arrest, and the first one to tweet about the incident in English. He posited that Twitter provides a different context for reporting "If you as a journalist don't use it, you do yourself a disservice as news breaks on Twitter, radio, television, newspaper—in that order."

However, despite all the positive arguments, Haffajee also points out that Twitter can be "a time and productivity drain" and that one has to be aware of the real value of time spent on Twitter as there is no line of revenue. Adding to the skills that Bateman showed us, journalists also need to be able to "discern between personal and professional views". Haffajee stated: "I am occasionally wild on Twitter and I've had to tame this voice because what I say here can be seen as the opinion of the newspaper."

Conclusions

One of the problems of social media research is that the research object is constantly in flux. Numbers of followers are changing significantly—and by the day. With data only from a specific position on the Twitter timeline, this sets certain limitations to the conclusions one can draw from a study such as the one explored in the present research. If your data are a snapshot, your conclusions will partly be as well. Secondly, while Twitter is an important social network that drives public debates, it is not identical with that debate as a single platform. However, using this platform as an indicator, we have tried to draw conclusions about South African journalists' Twitter relationships and the connections with the public debates.

The first impression from the South African Twitter 500 network is that its structure does not differ very much from journalists' networks on Twitter in the United Kingdom and The Netherlands (Verweij 2012b). A close examination of the structure of the South African Twitter network shows that it is composed of different groups, consisting of journalists from various media. Although the M&G takes up a strong position, and the top 20 on authority revealed a highly connected group, we concluded that neither of these two groups have complete control over the Twitter network; and further, based on the construction of various sub-groups, that the network has different solid centers and an open structure in which references to news source and news hounds are equally important. This pluralistic and open structure of the South African Twitter network is one of the important conditions for a space in which there is a free and open debate in South African society. Further, the role of the M&G and the top 20 on authority creates a strong platform for voicing and leading criticism and opposition.

Looking into three more detailed case studies, we concluded that the media and journalists on Twitter played a leading or central role in the debate. The role of the journalists was not limited to finding and bringing the news, but also extended to commenting and inviting the public to take part in topical discussions. Twitter, as a journalistic network, therefore strengthens the independence of public debate in a situation where the government aims at more control. The importance of this role of social networks like Twitter is growing in a situation where the government is trying to control the public debates through their "Protection of State Information Bill". The traditional media are easy to control, since they are centralized Controlling these media is, therefore, equal to controlling the source. Social media, however, are decentralized and, therefore, far more difficult to control by governments. Shutting down social—"we media"—as recent history in the Middle East has shown, is almost impossible.

Credibility is an important yardstick for judging the quality of news and reporting. Traditionally credibility was attached to the media houses and titles that journalists were representing. Twitter shows that journalists can now easily become "famous" as a brand unto themselves, where they are no longer related to the media house or title. The result of this could be that the role of individual journalists in public debates increases and that his/her credibility becomes an important condition for an open and independent public debate. On the other hand, the position of individual journalists as a brand in public debate could be weaker than journalists working for well-established media houses and newspaper titles. Whether this positive outlook on Twitter and the public debate is enough to escape the growing control of the South African government and their Information Bill remains to be seen.

NOTES

1. World Bank data (http://data.worldbank.org/country/south-africa) show the number of broadband networks.
2. For a Twitter list of 500 South African journalists, see http://hacks.mediahack.co.za/.
3. See http://hacks.mediahack.co.za/about.php.
4. "Twitterati" as used here refers to the "Tweet elite", whose 140-character tweets attract and capture the attention of thousands of followers. The term is part of a whole new vocabulary predominantly peculiar to the Twitter subculture.

REFERENCES

Baran, Stanley. 2011. *Introduction to Mass Communication*. London: McGraw Hill.

Bardoel, Jo. 2010. "De journalistiek moet zich durven onderscheiden." *Tijdschrift voor Communicatie* 38 (3): 232–241.

Bardoel, Jo and Mark Deuze. 2001. "Network Journalism: Converging Competences of Media Professionals and Professionalism." *Australian Journalism Review* 23: 91–103.

Castells, Manuel. 2000. *The Rise of the Network Society: the Information Age: Economy*. Society and Culture, New York: Wiley-Blackwell.

Cohen, Noam. 2009. "Twitter on the Barricades: Six Lessons Learned." The New York Times. Accessed September 12, 2013. http://www.nytimes.com/2009/06/21/weekinreview/21cohenweb.html?_r=0.

Farhi, Paul. 2009. "The Twitter Explosion." *The American Journalism Review*. June/July 2009.

Gans, Herbert J. 1980. *Deciding What's News NBC. A study of CBS Evening News Nightly News, Newsweek, and Time*. New York: Vintage Books.

Gillmor, Dan. 2004. *We the Media*. Sebastopol, CA: O'Reilly.

Guardian The, UK "*Journalists on Twitter:* How they Follow Each Other." Accessed September 12, 2013. http://www.guardian.co.uk/news/datablog/2011/apr/11/journalists-twitter-following.

Harbor, Anton and Margaret Renn, eds. 2010. *Troublemakers. The Best of South Africa's Investigative Journalism*. Johannesburg: Jacana Media.

Hansen, Derek L., Ben Shneiderman and Marc A. Smith. 2011. *Analyzing Social Media with NodeXL*. Amsterdam: Elsevier.

Hermida, Alfred. 2009. "*Twittering The News*. The emergence of ambient journalism." *Journalism Practice* 4 (3): 297–308.

Hirst, Tony. 2011. Visualizing Twitter Friend Connections Using Gephi. http://blog.ouseful.info/2011/07/07/visualising-twitter-friend-connections-using-gephi-an-example-using-wireduk-friends-network/.

Huberman, B. A., D. M. Romero, and W. Fang. 2009. "Social networks that matter: Twitter under the microscope." *First Monday* 14 (1). http://firstmonday.org/ojs/index.php/fm/article/view/2317/2063

Luyendijk, Joris. 2010. *Je hebt het niet van mij, maar .... Podium*, Amsterdam.

Meyer, Philip. 2004. *The Vanishing Newspaper*. Saving Journalism in the Information Age: University of Missouri Press.

Pew Research Center. 2011, November 14. How mainstream media outlets use Twitter. http://pewresearch.org/pubs/2130/twitter-news-organizations.

Rosen, Jay. 2012. What's Different (Really Different) about the Web. http://pressthink.org, Lecture at Expert day NVJ, Amsterdam. http://www.slideshare.net/peterverweij/rosen-expertday-pdf.

Verweij, Peter. 2010. *Twitter as a Source for Journalists*. Paper WJEC Rhodes University. http://wjec.ru.ac.za/.

Verweij, Peter. 2012a. How Data Can save Journalism as We Know It. http://memeburn.com/2012/10/how-data-can-save-journalism-as-we-know-it/.

Verweij, Peter. 2012b. "Twitter Links Between Politicians and Journalists." *Journalism Practice* 6 (5–6): 680–691.

Verweij, Peter. 2013a. Twitter Geeft de Indivualisering van de Journalistiek een Zetje. http://www.denieuwereporter.nl/2013/03/twitter-geeft-de-individualisering-van-de-journalistiek-een-zetje/.

Verweij, Peter. 2013b. Twitter Journalism: Lessons from #OscarPistorius. http://d3-media.blogspot.nl/2013/02/twitter-journalism-lessons-from.html.

Wakita, K. and T. Tsurumi. 2007. "Finding Community Structure in Mega Scale Social Networks." In Proceedings of the 16th International Conference on the World Wide Web. Banff, Alberta. Canada, May 2007.

Wasserman, Stanley, and Faust., Katherine. 1994. *Social Network Analysis: Methods and Applications*. Cambridge: Cambridge University Press.

WorldWideWorx. 2012. South Africa breaks barriers in SA. http://www.worldwideworx.com/socialmedia2012/.

Index